My Two New Hearts:

How An Intimate Journey With Jesus Gave me Peace Through Life's Toughest Hardships

BILL JERNIGAN

ISBN:10: 0999773100
ISBN-13:978-0999773109

DEDICATION

This book is dedicated to my Lord and Savior Jesus Christ whose indescribable and unmeasurable love made possible my two new hearts.

I also acknowledge the efforts and love of my family and friends who walked through the trials of my life with understanding, love and a great deal of prayer.

The Diaz family of Laredo Texas
The entire Diaz family made a great gift to me, their son Rudy's heart that I may continue to live. There is not a gift anyone on earth could give me that means as much as their love. They are part of our family and our family theirs.

This book is also dedicated to all of the deeply loving, warm and compassionate nurses, doctors, technicians and support personnel at the Center for Advanced Heart Failure and Memorial Hermann Hospital, Heart Vascular Institute of the Texas Medical Center, Houston, Texas.

To all who changed bandages, hung IVs, check wounds, kept a constant vigil on my progress and listened to my goofy sense of human, you made life a wonderful journey.

Without God's provision of the new heart and the loving care I received this part of my life, new or old, would not have meant as much.

I Love you all,
Bill Jernigan

CONTENTS

ACKNOWLEDGMENTS

"My Two New Hearts"

A title suggested by my friend, Mark Markle

Cover Art Work

I wish to thank my brother Larry for the painting ("Cœur à Cœur – le Cercle de la Vie" (Heart to Heart The Circle of Life) which is on display in the 25th floor of Memorial Hermann's Center for Advanced Heart Failure. He is a wonderful artist and his wife Lisa has to put up with him and his co-conspirator in crime, me.

Two other people have helped make this work possible, Mark Page and Linda Winder. They have poured over and over the manuscript for errors and mistakes. Linda use to be an English teacher. You should have seen my first draft. She wore out her red pen.

His painting reminds me of his of love for me and the generosity of the donor family for the gift of their son's heart. Recently Karen and I traveled to meet the entire family face-to-face and took a stethoscope for the family to hear their son's heart still beating. Our two families are truly intertwined.

INTRODUCTION

Think, at the age of thirty-three your physician telling you, "You have had a heart attack. " What a shocker! I can only confess to you that this was a time of deep depression and questioning, "Will my life be like that of my mother who had heart attacks, by-pass surgeries and death at the age of fifty-seven? What was my life going to be like? Would I be an invalid? What would happen to my family?

That fateful day was August 8, 1988. Twenty-eight years later on August 8, 2016 I was in the heart catheter lab. I noticed the date; it was August 8, 2016.

The level of weeping in thanksgiving was enormous. To think − the Lord has kept me through these health issues for nearly 28 years. The very situation where my mother had died I live! I have no doubt, what-so-ever; The Lord Jesus' hand has been upon my life. What's mind boggling is His degree of love and care for my life.

My journey has shaken me to the bedrock of my spirit. To think that Jesus is the only one who has died for me and in that death gave me a new heart. Now to know someone died for me to live. Many try to dismiss this in that the donor will be giving a special gift. Yes, but he will still have to die.

Have you ever truly wondered what goes through a person's mind knowing whether they live or die is left up to the Lord God? I offer my experiences through my life facing the trials and tribulations of life and more important than anything - watching God work out the details. My walk with Him has made it possible to face each day, whether knowing the outcome or not. That's faith.

My hope is to make this story more than a sterile set of facts, but an encouragement to each reader to trust Jesus with every aspect of their life. It is easy to trust the Father when life is going well, but it is a different matter to patiently await His answers when life is falling apart.

You will see my struggles, and how God addressed each situation in my life. My prayer is that each one who reads this work will be encouraged to live their life wholly and entirely for the God who loves you and I more than we could ever image.

I have to begin with a passage of Scriptures that could relate everything I have to say:

> " 'Jesus said, 'No one can serve two masters; for either he will hate the one and love the other, or he will be devoted to one and despise the other. You cannot serve God and wealth. [25] For this reason I say to you, do not be worried about your life, as to what you will eat or what you will drink; nor for your body, as to what you will put on. Is not life more than food, and the body more than clothing? [26] Look at the birds of the air, that they do not sow, nor reap nor gather into barns, and yet your heavenly Father feeds them. Are you not worth much more than they? [27] And who of you by being worried can add a single hour to his life? [28] And why are you worried about clothing? Observe how the lilies of the field grow; they do not toil nor do they spin, [29] yet I say to you that not even Solomon in all his glory clothed himself like one of these. [30] But if God so clothes the grass of the field, which is alive today and tomorrow is thrown into the furnace, will He not much more clothe you? You of little faith! [31] Do not worry then, saying, What will we eat? or What will we drink? or What will we wear for clothing? [32] For the Gentiles eagerly seek all these things; for your heavenly Father knows that you need all these things. [33] But seek first His kingdom and His righteousness, and all these things will be added to you. [34] So do not worry about tomorrow; for tomorrow will care for itself. Each day has enough trouble of its own.' " (Matthew 6:24-34)

I felt led to use this passage for one reason only. Too many people inside the church fellowship and outside the redemption family seem to be too concerned with their needs of life.

These concerned people spend an extraordinary amount of time worrying or heavily concerned with the needs of their life, including, but not limited to: health issues, raising children, paying bills, intimacy and many more.

The point of this passage and these concerns is trust. Can we trust Jesus with every aspect of life or not? Does our Heavenly Father truly love us or not? If a person is to live in peace, one has to completely and totally accept the fact that God Almighty loves us, His children, more than we can ever image or measure.

My lifetime has been spent discovering the depths of God's love and His provisions for my life. There have been times when I have doubted His love. Every time I have doubted God's love I have actually found myself in a self-imposed pity party. While I haven't verbalized the following words, "Woe is me!" they have actually been my internal sentiment.

REASON FOR THIS BOOK

I have written this book first, because I felt a deep conviction from the Lord to help people suffering through life's difficulties. Secondly is to help people understand how one's trust in the Lord and dependence upon Him can bring peace to an otherwise troubled life.

MAY THE PEACE OF THE LORD
RULE IN YOUR HEART AND LIFE

Unless otherwise indicated, all Scriptures are from the New American Standard Bible (NASB)

1 LIFE BEFORE MY FIRST NEW HEART

Defining what a "new heart" means:

Let me define the "first new heart". It is the transplant of the heart of God's Son, Jesus into my life.

> "Now because you are his children, God has sent the Spirit of his Son into our hearts to cry out, 'Abba! Father!'" (Galatians 4:6, NIV)

> "And the peace of God, which transcends all understanding, will guard your hearts and your minds in Christ Jesus." (Philippians 4:7, NIV)

The first new heart the Scriptures identify is the spiritual heart. The Jewish perspective of Jesus' day, the heart was the center of understanding and commitment. In both the Old and New Testaments, God wanted His children to have His Word and live in a loving relationship with Him.

> "I will give you a new heart and put a new spirit in you; I will remove from you your heart of stone and give you a heart of flesh. [27] And I will put my Spirit in you and move you to follow my decrees and be careful to keep my laws." (Ezekiel 36:26-27, NIV)

> "You show that you are a letter from Christ, the result of our ministry, written not with ink but with the Spirit of the living God, not on tablets of stone but on tablets of human hearts." (2 Corinthians 3:3, NIV)

Our modern perspective of the heart leads us to understand the heart with two functions: distributing blood throughout the body but also the center of our emotions. Living in a covenant relationship with Almighty God is both emotional (worship) and commitment (obedience). Too often we put emphasis on the feeling without the commitment and or obedience.

What does God want? He desires that we understand and implement His Word in our lives. The Lord God wants our heart-felt, committed love and appreciation of Him.

Through the redemption process, Jesus gives the new believer His heart so we might live successfully in the Kingdom of God. This process of rebirth and rejuvenation causes us to abandon our old ways in favor of Jesus' ways. But too often people try to straddle the fence and live in both worlds. This idea is as foreign as living without a heart. Jesus said,

> "To the angel of the church in Laodicea write: These are the words of the Amen, the faithful and true witness, the ruler of God's creation. [15] I know your deeds, that you are neither cold nor hot. I wish you were either one or the other! [16] So, because you are lukewarm—neither hot nor cold—I am about to spit you out of my mouth. [17] You say, 'I am rich; I have acquired wealth and do not need a thing.' But you do not realize that you are wretched, pitiful, poor, blind and naked." (Revelation 3:14-17, NIV)

One should be able to plainly see, that one cannot live in two different worlds, the spiritual (eternal) and physical (natural). One of the choices will suffer resulting in a world of spiritual confusion for the person.

My family of influence

Neither my dad nor mom was spiritually minded. Like many others, they were busy making a living for the family and a mere existence. They did teach their children moral concepts, such as, do not steal and do not lie, but they were neither regular worshippers of the Living God nor did they actively pursue a relationship with Jesus.

On the other hand, my maternal grandmother was a funny, lively and truly godly woman who tried her best to teach her grandchildren about living under the Lordship of Christ. Nanny, as we called her, would read me stories out of the Bible and discuss the meaning of the Scriptures. This loving woman was probably the largest contributor to me receiving my first new heart – the heart of Christ.

Our parents loved us very much. Like many other adults of the World War II generation, they had the attitude of providing for their children beyond what they themselves received during their childhood. They provided a nice home, autos for each child and many other typical family benefits, but what we would need for eternity was not there.

Their lives were centered in business. They owned, managed and worked long, hard days and the business was successful, but we had little family life. Our life revolved around the business too.

My three siblings, Joe, Larry, Sheila and myself, grew up in this restaurant business. My dad would start us off at the bottom, dishwashing. Sheila helped the wait staff and I was the cashier. While dishwashing, Larry became very interested in food. He was often caught eating the food the cook prepared for a customer. Scraps? There were none! I won't tell you the nickname Sheila gave Larry. But outside of school, every evening was spent in the family business.

<u>My adolescent life</u>

Center, Texas was and probably still is, not completely in sync with the outside world. Things come to Center a little later than most towns. When I left for college, I was surprised at what I did not know and everyone else did.

But, as a person that grew up in the late 1960's and early 1970's, rock n' roll finally made it to Center. My friends were listening to Jimi Hendrix, and many others. We had a "youth center" which was supposed to give the youth of the community some place to go and something to do. We'd go to dances or on off nights, play pool. The "youth center" was more of a place to hook up with someone who had booze or weed. Obviously, I was exposed to a great deal of worldly influences. This was a time of the beginning of the "free love revolution", the exposure to weed, as well as rock and roll. If one was not centered in a walk with Jesus, one was almost certainly doomed to make a huge list of mistakes as most youth even today.

There were many areas of this society I fell into. This writer was not a perfect, loving and Christ-like person. My language was corrupted, my morals would be considered dishonoring of God and my desires were only of earthly rewards and fulfillment. I would be ashamed to tell you what my life was truly like. But understand this – my life was not too different from the life of an unredeemed person of today. I was a heathen!

My life was centered on "me". Later I discovered this is called narcissism or self-centeredness. Whatever benefited me is what I did. My belief system was heavily influenced by my own motives and what satisfied my desires.

My early adulthood life

Life for me in this period was only a further spiraling growth of my adolescent years. I was free, living outside the eyes of my parents and no one could tell me the consequences of my living. I did and went as I pleased.

This time was also a time of experimentation and exploration in relationships. Relationships with women were casual and uncommitted. A number of years later I realized what I sought were meaningful relationships.

My prayer for you right now is this, "Heavenly Father, I know what You delivered me from and what You have done in my life and whatever You need to do in the life of the reader of this work, please manifest yourself in power, in Your love and Your victory for Your name's sake. Amen."

The point of this chapter is to show you that, like most people in America I had a previous life before Jesus saved me. This life was normal for the world, but soon I was to discover my own reality and eventually my own mortality, but beyond description, I am humbly grateful to the Lord God for saving me through His Son, Jesus.

2 MY FIRST NEW HEART

In 1977, the Executive Vice President of a bank invited me to go to work for his bank. I accepted the job, never realizing all that might befall me.

But there was a co-worker who had a young, beautiful daughter. One day I saw her picture and had the strongest desire to meet her. I asked where she worked and her mother told me at the bank down the street. A good friend was an officer at this bank, so under the disguise of conducting banking business I went by and asked for the young lady to wait on me. She was all I expected and more. Our first two or three dates were supervised, either by her mother or my friend. Later I was told this was an escape mechanism besides, she could not remember my last name. A couple of years later Karen and I were married. We have now been married for over three decades and have two great children and a grand-daughter. This event was what I call my first "Divine Appointment" – a godly wife.

Three years passed and an older co-worker, Eilene, whom I loved as a sister invited me to her church. I attended Memorial Baptist Church in Port Arthur, Texas. One week the church held an old fashioned revival and I attended. One of the evenings I began to sense the seriousness of sin upon my life. I remember weeping, almost uncontrollably, over the weight of my sin. I knew my life was in danger if I didn't make a response, so that evening I prayed to receive Jesus as my Lord and Savior and dedicated my life to Him and His purpose. That evening was the time I received my first heart. Christ began to change my priorities, my language, my friends and my outlook on life. You've heard of a total makeover? Jesus did a radical spiritual make over. This according to Scriptures is called "transformation". Jesus gave me my first new heart, a spiritual one. My first new heart was a gift from Christ.

This event began the evening I prayed to the Father for the forgiveness of my sins, to be cleansed from all unrighteousness and that night I gave my life to Christ.

The first "Divine Appointment" was an appointment with God's only Son, Jesus Christ.

Most people are like donuts. What is the common design of a donut? A hole. A donut without a hole is just a blob of round dough, usually called a "filled" donut.

God created us with our own insufficiency or hole and left us to make a choice, to accept His guiding and loving presence or not. Our insufficiency leaves us with a crucial need – we need God's Son, Jesus to fill our lives with the hope and victory of the cross through His redemption. This decision to be filled with Christ's presence is a voluntary decision.

Once Christ rules our life, He fills in our insufficiencies, our weakest moments, the need for meaningful relationships and provides a brand new heart that is focused on Him. He filled with His peace and a love that fills our hearts with a warmth unavailable to the earthly man.

I neither believe in accidents nor luck, but prefer to see events in light of "Divine Appointments". A "Divine Appointment" is much like any appointment one might set. There is the time of meeting together with an outcome. In the case of "Divine Appointment" there is the arrangement that God has made to show you and I His great love and provision for us and to invite us to join Him in what He is doing. This is a time of discovering the deeper mysteries of God.

"He made known to us the mystery of His will, according to His good pleasure that He planned in Him." (Ephesians 1:9, HCSB)

The mysteries of God are unlimited in number and power. These mysteries are available to everyone, but God chooses to reveal His mysteries only to His children who are receptive and responsive. These folks are the recipient of God's truth and mysteries because they are ready for the truth and God knows they will use the revelation of the mystery for His glory.

I mention this teaching for an important reason, because many in and outside the church do not know His biblical truths. We have a deep need to know the Father and His truths.

In September 1981, the Heavenly Father made another "Divine Appointment when Karen and I were married. She had been raised in the faith community of a Baptist church and I wasn't. She was much more familiar with Scriptures and faith than I was. We both were intermittently faithful to Sunday School and worship and as we both grew in our spiritual walk, we grew closer together.

Meanwhile, in November 1982 we were given a gift of a beautiful son, Sean. Becoming parents is a challenge. My focus, like many men, was on career. I have come to see this is a mistake in many men's lives - career first, family second and God third. This was me.

Shortly after my commitment to Christ, my mother passed away with advance heart failure at the age of fifty-seven. I don't remember anyone expressing shock because of her long illness. What we did experience was mourning. This was a time when the family had to rally around my dad.

My dad took Mom's death hard. While he knew of her illness I don't believe a spouse is ever ready for the other's death.

Mom died six weeks after the birth of our oldest child, Sean. Since Mom was so frail, we didn't make a lot of demands on my parents. She saw Sean shortly after birth, but never held him. This is something that still today makes me sad.

Six weeks after my mother passed away, my little sister, Sheila and two others went missing while fishing off the jetties of Sabine Pass. The U.S. Coast Guard and several other agencies made extensive searches. She was never found and presumed dead.

My two brothers, Joe, the oldest and Larry, the youngest along with myself, seemed to be devastated by the two deaths, our mom and sister, so close together. I have to admit our dad never got over Sheila's death. In fact many times in the privacy of a father and son time, he would ask me, "Do you really think Sheila is dead?"

This was a time of searching for significance in my profession as a banker. I found myself restless and longing to fly up the corporate banking ladder of success and income. We had moved from Port Arthur, Texas to Nacogdoches, but this relocation was not satisfying to me. There was still something missing. We moved to the exciting Metroplex (Dallas/Ft. Worth area) and lived in a small town, Rowlett, about twelve miles east of Dallas.

For the next few years life went on. Karen and I were involved in Bible study and worship, but we experienced minimum spiritual growth. You may understand that while churches are working hard to accomplish Jesus' mandate of bringing people into the Kingdom of God, many find it difficult to truly disciple or train new believers. This problem is not entirely the churches' fault because as I've already mentioned many times young adults are focused on many things that draw them away from the true importance – their relationship with the Heavenly Father.

God had given me a new spiritual heart, but His church did not fill my life with life-building teaching that would anchor me to Jesus and give me success in life and a ministry to serve my God. This fact later gave me a passion to fill others' lives with that which I had not received.

We had moved to Rowlett to accept a Vice Presidency in lending. I believe this was a time when God gave Karen and me our next "Divine Appointment". After three years in Rowlett, banks began to collapse in Texas. I was suddenly unemployed. After many months of searching from California to New York and seeing no response, my Pastor said to me one day, "Bill, I have never seen someone send more resumes and have no responses. I think God has something very special in mind for you."

I now found I had time to help our youth minister touch the lives of our youth. I enjoyed it deeply and found that God was using this to grow me spiritually. Not knowing what was happening, one Sunday morning I walked the aisle and told our Pastor I felt a strong urging of the Holy Spirit to surrender to the ministry. Let me give you my definition of surprise: the look on our Pastor's face and the look on my wife's face when they heard my thoughts. I had not told anyone of what was stirring in my spirit.

We later moved to my hometown, Center, Texas, where my dad lived. This was a farming community, a town I later called Mayberry. My dad asked me to help him with the business side of a restaurant he was opening. He was operational and I was the business person. A year goes by and the restaurant failed. Once again, I was unemployed.

The Lord provided both Karen and I with jobs. Karen went to work for the county agent and she seemed to have the time of her life. Someone introduced me to Pastor Mark. Mark is a man my own age, but he had already been in the ministry for twenty years. We began spiritual conversations and prayer as well as a more personal and informal time of discipleship. Our families became good friends. He and I worked on several ministry projects and

Mark helped me grasp the idea of putting together a Bible study and sermon. Mark became a mentor in Christ, a brother in the labor and a friend in life who remains precious to me even now.

Mark is a practical man. If someone needed food, he fed them. If they needed some job done, he did it. He helped me get a job at a church several miles away on the grounds crew. While working at this church the Lord continued working on my attitude, my speech and my priorities. In addition, I learned more about people and taking care of God's property.

My lunch hours became very precious to me, possibly the most precious personal time I had ever had. It was so unfortunate that I only had one hour, but God and I met at a picnic bench every day. I learned so much. Independently, the Father began to fill my new heart with His eternal truths. **His presence in my life brought more to me than I had to offer Him.**

While in Center, we served at First Baptist Church, Center. Our Pastor, Ken, arrived in Center a year or so prior to our arrival. Ken had a missionary spirit. In fact Pastor Ken and his wife would eventually go as missionaries to Africa. The Lord's influence in his life impacted everyone in the church and especially Karen and me. Ken's deep conviction about the church's spiritual renewal drove his ministry.

During this time we experienced the Spirit of God move through that church and our lives. There were many studying "Experiencing God: Knowing and Doing the Will of God," by Henry Blackaby. I discovered what spiritual growth was and God was doing a major work of disciple-making and growing both Karen and myself. This would be a time that would influence the rest of my personal life and ministry life.

The surrendering to ministry wasn't a wasted effort. The longing I had a couple of years earlier was still alive and even stronger. Karen and I continued to pray about what God wanted us to do.

God began revealing His will for my life. There were two competing emotions: wonder and awe. My experience of wonder was built upon the fact that God was calling me into His ministry. I asked, "How can this be? Doesn't He know what my life's been like?" "I am not a Moses or some Old or New Testament person." The awe came from the fact that I realized how much God truly loves me and how He wanted His best for me.

My home church licensed me to the ministry. The Father gave me a deep sense that I needed more spiritual training, which is called discipleship. Have you ever heard of a minister that didn't know the depths of the Bible? New Orleans Baptist Theological Seminary had classes at a local church in Shreveport, Louisiana. The classes were like sopping gravy with a biscuit. Soooo good! So filling!

A few short weeks go by and a small country church (Antioch) asked me to be their Pastor. There my spiritual training or discipleship continued through the lessons from the people and the trials and tribulations of leadership. I often laugh when I remember a statement our deacon chairman shared one day.

> "There's the right way. There's the wrong way, and there is the Antioch way."

God the Father awards every genuine new follower of Jesus, His Son, with a new spiritual heart. One hundred sixty-five verses in the New Testament alone discuss the need, the importance, and the effect of our spiritual heart, for example:

> Matthew 5:8 "Blessed are the pure in heart, for they shall see God."

Jesus addressed a crucial need for every human being to receive a new heart:

Matthew 5:28; 6:21; 9:4; 12:34; 13:15; 15:18-19; 19:8

Discipleship for a believer can come from different directions, different people, but never-the-less, God gives a new heart to those who seriously surrender their life to His Son, Jesus.

The foremost benefit and result of a new heart is found in the Old and New Testament

"And He (Jesus) said to him, 'You shall love the Lord your God with all your heart, and with all your soul, and with all your mind. This is the great and foremost commandment.'" (Matthew 22:37)

"Peace I leave with you; My peace I give to you; not as the world gives do I give to you. Do not let your heart be troubled, nor let it be fearful." (John 14:27)

"And the congregation of those who believed were of one heart and soul; and not one of them claimed that anything belonging to him was his own, but all things were common property to them."(Acts 4:32)

God's gift of a new heart can turn a person's life into a worth-while life if allowed. Jesus replaced despair with joy. He turned my hurt into healing, and defeat into victory. Radically, the Holy Spirit began to redirect my life into understanding God's truth and implementing God's truth. He turned my self-centeredness into caring for others. He turned my need to always be right into an attitude of "I don't know it all." God the Father sustained and invigorated our marriage.

My first new heart provided all I would ever need and goes way beyond what I could ever expect.

3 HOW MY FIRST NEW HEART
CHANGED MY LIFE

Everyone has heard claims "it will change your life." People peddling cookware, wrinkle remover, denture cream and pain relievers all claim "it will change your life." There's even a local bank that makes the same claim on their outdoor sign.

These claims are like a Mary Poppin's statement, "a pie shell promise, easily made and easily broken". The true test of "change" is the depth and difference it has made in one's life. Most of the products that make these promises are like the Nineteenth Century's snake oil salesmen that traveled around the countryside making wild claims to innocent and unsuspecting consumers.

Throughout the years I have known many people who have had their lives totally transformed by the living presence of Jesus Christ in their lives. Transformation is measured in long-range of time, not a short-range of time. I have personally witnessed people who have claimed to have a transformation to live their life for a season or two, but eventually their lives falls apart, they return to their old ways before the "religious experience" and rejected their faith and Christ.

The word transformation comes from a Greek word, "metamorphosis". Metamorphosis is what happens when a caterpillar spins a cocoon around its body. It then goes into hibernation and while in the cocoon becomes a totally different creature. It enters a worm and exits a beautiful butterfly.

Like the need for by-pass surgery or heart transplant changes are slowly made in the body over time. The new heart Jesus gave me when I became a child of God slowly began to show its effect. Priorities transitioned. Passions changed. Personal relationships became built on a faith community.

After surrendering to the ministry in 1991 and being ordained I sensed a great need for a theological education. If I were going to be a minister I needed to have an understanding of Scriptures and ministry. So our family left our lives behind in East Texas. Our extended family and friends were seen in the rear view mirror as we left the familiar homeland of East Texas for an unknown, foreign land of New Orleans.

I sadly, deeply and affectionately remember putting the finishing touches cleaning the house we were moving out of to go to New Orleans. My dad and I were cleaning the kitchen and as we stood at the kitchen sink, he said, "I feel like this is good-bye." I can only tell you how I thought about this all the drive to New Orleans in a U-Haul. The thought bewildered me. I asked myself, "What did he mean?"

A year later I realized what my dad meant. He was admitted to the hospital with advanced heart failure. We would see each other a few times between our move to New Orleans and his death, but visits were seldom and far between. I felt as though he was saying that moving day, "This is it! We won't be around each other as we have been throughout the years. On the other hand, he did say that he understood and respected me for making the decision to go into ministry.

God led us to New Orleans Baptist Theological seminary and there I completed my undergraduate degree in biblical and pastoral studies. When we arrived on campus, neither Karen nor I had jobs. We went on shear faith that God had led us there and He would provide. He did.

There were countless times God confirmed our presence studying His Word and preparing for ministry. Within a couple of weeks of arriving in New Orleans we both had jobs on campus, Karen in the Registrar's Office and me in guest housing. We worked and attended classes on campus where we could be close to our children. We were within a minute of our children. who went to school a couple of blocks away and played with our seminary students' kids in our cloistered neighborhood. We were able to develop long-lasting and deep relationships from fellow students, faculty and administration.

In seminary, students would get into all types of discussions. One brother stated that the very instant he accepted Jesus as Lord and Savior, his life completely and thoroughly changed. At first I had a problem with his statement and then I realized I was interpreting what he said through my own life. Change for me was gradual, but powerful.

I have to tell you a story to make sense of the two different. My dad was a merchant seaman for twenty-eight years. When he retired, he was the ship's quartermaster. His job was to steer the ship, keeping it on course toward the intended port.

Now this man could steer a 750 foot ship, but he could not maneuver a sixteen-foot bass boat. One day we were on the lake fishing and while headed to shore, he ran the boat upon the bank at a full throttle. There were two men sitting on the pier having to hold their sides laughing so hard. Initially I didn't laugh, but strangely enough my dad never laughed about the situation. It was an embarrassment for him.

The point is this: it takes much longer and farther to make a U-turn in large vessel than in a small one. I asked my dad how long it takes to make a U-turn in a huge ship. He said miles and miles. Could it be that the U-turn or total transformation in our lives takes different amounts of time and energy for different people? My belief is that it does. God is the one that is responsible for making changes in our lives, but He does have to deal with our free-choice. God has to maneuver through the mine fields we have set up. He has to overcome our prejudices and idiosyncrasies.

Never the less, God still expects ever person who claims to be His to be transformed or experience a total life metamorphosis into the image of His Son, Jesus.

"God….. He chose them us to be like his Son so that Jesus." (Romans 8:29, NCV)

"He also predestined us to be conformed to the image of His Son." (Romans 8:29, KJV)

Regardless of what religious background one comes from all Scriptures have the same application. God expects us all to be like a ship always making a coarse correction of repentance and spiritual growth toward Jesus, His Son.

Have you ever thought that "going to church" was boring, useless, or impractical? I once thought that, too. However, the spiritual new heart can and will change this attitude. Jesus gives us a thought in the transformation of the heart from the spiritually dull to the spiritually alive. He said, "Seek first the Kingdom of God and His righteousness" (Matthew 6:33)

While the preceding verses have to do with basic human needs of food, clothing, there is also another thought. When one seeks God with all their heart, one will find Him. He is close by and listening to your prayer.

"You will seek the LORD your God, and you will Find Him if you search for Him with all your heart and all your soul."(Deuteronomy 4:29)

Moses is a good example of a person with a new heart. In Exodus, one day he realized he wasn't Egyptian, but rather a Hebrew. As he looked down from his high place of honor as Pharaoh's daughter's son, he saw his own people suffering under the pain and agony of the Egyptian task masters' whips. His own people were being beaten, maimed, starved and mistreated.

We are told, in Exodus chapter two, verse 11 that Moses saw an Egyptian mistreating a Hebrew slave. He went out and confronted the Egyptian, struck him and buried him in the sand. When Pharaoh learned of this event he committed to having Moses killed, but Moses fled to Midian.

After marrying Jethro's daughter Zipporah, Moses became a shepherd serving his father-in-law. While in the desert near Mt. Horeb (also known as Sinai) the Lord appeared in the form of a burning bush that wasn't consumed. You think you know someone who is curious. Beside the word curious in Webster's Dictionary is Moses' picture. His curiosity got the best of him and he ascended the mountain to see this amazing event. "[3] So Moses said, 'I must turn aside now and see this marvelous sight, why the bush is not burned up.' [4] When the LORD saw that he turned aside to look, God called to him from the midst of the bush and said, 'Moses, Moses!' And he said, 'Here I am.' (Exodus 3:3–4)

In the midst of Moses' life, he responded to God seeking him. In verse 2, "the Angel" is the Lord. Remember Deuteronomy 4:29? When you seek the Lord, you will find Him if you search with all your heart and all your soul.

Many people only seek God after their life has gone totally out of control. In many ways Moses' life spiraled from a favored son of Egypt to the lowly life of a shepherd in the desert, stinking like sheep.

Karen and I had been bankers. Life for us had a lot of certainty and routine. We enjoyed a lifestyle that included going to professional football, baseball, and basketball games with important people from and related to our bank. Customers would often take us out for lunch or dinner. Life was comfortable and enjoyable, that is until one fateful day when the bank was put under the control of F.D.I.C. officials and began to take over our bank for illegal loan activity. Many employed by the bank were suddenly unemployed. Many banks in Louisiana, Oklahoma and Texas were being singled out for bad lending practices. Many innocent people suffered right alongside those who made the bad decisions.

Life in our family all of a sudden became one-hundred eighty degrees from what it had been. Instead of being safe and secure in our jobs and life-style, we were thrust into uncertainty and near poverty. We had once lived within our means, now we struggled to buy groceries. We had to surrender our home and rent an apartment. Instead of working one job each, we now had two or three jobs each. Karen worked at her full-time job plus a fast food chain. I worked for a grocery store and a hardware store as a clerk, and a doctor's office filing insurance claims. This period seemed to last forever.

During this time, I suffered my first heart attack. August 8, 1988 was a pivotal day in our lives. Everyone was astonished. I saw my dad standing over me in ICU with worry upon his face because His son was suffering from the same ailment that took his wife (my mother) six years earlier.

I cannot tell you what it is like to have a heart attack at the age of 33. Two nights prior to the first attack, I woke up about 2 a.m. asking Karen to rub my upper left back and shoulder because the pain was so unbearable. The morning of heart attack number 1, I went to the doctor's office and he pronounced me healthy as a mule. I drove to downtown Dallas to go to work and about 1 pm with the pain so intense, I drove 12 miles back home to the doctor's office. Upon arrival the doctor chewed me out for driving that far and asked his wife to drive me to the E.R. The next day all blood test were in and think about it. At the age of thirty-three your physician telling you, "You have had a heart attack!"

Each consecutive visit to the E.R. for this problem was as difficult as the first. Doctors simply did not believe or understand how a healthy looking person with a young family can be having or have had a heart attack. I finally developed a response, "I have had them before, don't you think I know what it feels like?"

Depression and anger temporarily ruled my day. I truly do not know why. Was I angry at God? Was I angry at myself? I could only imagine the worst. Yet, I healed quite quickly and completely.

A nurse asked me, "Do you know how lucky you are? Men who have heart attacks at the age of 33 do not live to say good-bye to their families." Instantly I knew what God had done. Instead of ending my life or allowing me to be in some vegetative state, I would live normally, except for a new diet. No ice cream! No fried foods! Low-fat everything! I translated "low-fat" from the ancient Babylonian. It means "NO TASTE!"

Life did not get any easier. While I was and am a child of the King and my citizenship is not of this earth, but in Heaven, I know who holds my life in His hands, there is still life. Life itself has a way of getting in the middle of our plans, our aspirations, and desires. To make a story shorter, this was the first heart attack of eight. Each one hurt like crazy, but unlike attack number one – I began to understand the Heavenly Father more each time.

My second heart attack and resulting by-pass surgery occurred while I was taking my last class on the graduate side of seminary. Once again I thought of my mother and her journey of heart attacks and by-pass surgeries. After surgery I felt great. The only physical challenge was regaining strength from the surgery.

Heart attacks became a double-sided coin: one side was a painful and uncertain in timing and the other side was a celebration for God's deliverance. These eight attacks were always a major interruption to life and my plans.

Each consecutive event would leave me with questions, but soon I began to see a pattern: attack and God moved in my life. The pattern became obvious to Karen and me both. Each time, God made major moves in our lives and never what we expected, nor did we take these situations for granted.

Have you ever faced a situation and thought you had learned the lesson, only later to discover that you hadn't? Each heart event not only led me to a deeper understanding of who God is and His great love and compassion for the humans He created, but gave me a deeper understanding and meaning of biblical faith.

My lesson I want to pass on to everyone is this: God doesn't promised us a tomorrow on earth, but He does promise to be with us every moment of the day and every day of our life. The other lesson, from Scriptures I learned in my own life – each day is a gift from God. Never waste it or not be thankful for it.

I was able to celebrate God's provision of life, in light of each event and realization that He has delivered me for a reason. Each encounter was a fresh reminder of His love and provision for me. These were times of discovering deeper truths and mysteries of God.

How can anyone celebrate tragedy, pain?

"And we rejoice in the hope of the glory of God. [3] Not only so, but we also rejoice in our sufferings, because we know that suffering produces perseverance; [4] perseverance, character; and character, hope. [5] And hope does not disappoint us, because God has poured out his love into our hearts by the Holy Spirit, whom he has given us." (Romans 5:2-5)

"For I consider that the sufferings of this present time are not worthy to be compared with the glory that is to be revealed to us." (Romans 8:8)

"Blessed be the God and Father of our Lord Jesus Christ, who according to His great mercy has caused us to be born again to a living hope through the resurrection of Jesus Christ from the dead, [4] to obtain an inheritance which is imperishable and undefiled and will not fade away, reserved in heaven for you, [5] who are protected by the power of God through faith for a salvation ready to be revealed in the last time. [6] In this you greatly rejoice, even though now for a little while, if necessary, you have been distressed by various trials, [7] so that the proof of your faith, being more precious than gold which is perishable, even though tested by fire, may be found to result in praise and glory and honor at the revelation of Jesus Christ; [8] and though you have not seen Him, you love Him, and though you do not see Him now, but believe in Him, you greatly rejoice with joy inexpressible and full of glory' [9] obtaining as the outcome of your faith the salvation of your souls." (1 Peter 1:3-9)

Does this mean we become ecstatically happy when we suffer? No, we become reconciled to the fact that all human beings suffer from one source or another, but not from the Father. What should not be there is remorse, guilt (unless it is of our own making) with despair and defeat. I found I am victorious, not defeated. The

Lord God has provided for me through every event in my life and each time I slumped in faith, He picked me up, dusted me off and said, "It will be all right, son." He is the only one that can make that promise!

After looking back, the Lord's leading us to First Baptist Church; Center was our next "Divine Appointment". Our Pastor's journey would have repercussions upon the entire church. Ken had made a connection with Henry Blackaby prior to the famous Bible study's publication. Henry preached revival at First, Center for two straight years. He would introduce totally new spiritual concepts for this small-town, county seat, died-in-the-wool sleepy, traditional church that probably had not seen any stirring of the Lord in two or three decades.

Lunch was a divine encounter every day. I would take my Bible, my study book and my lunch to a park. There I would encounter my bologna sandwich and God's Word. It is surprising how much spiritual growth can occur when one takes one's lunch and dedicates that time to the Lord. This time became so special! I felt as though I had lunch with God Almighty every day. I heard someone say in discipleship class one day, "God told me….." My silent question was, "God speaks to you? How? What does He say?" My time with the Lord in the park began to settle this question and I came to understand what she meant. God speaks! Looking back in life, I have discovered if we listen He will speak to us!

As I grew in the Lord, I realized how much He loves me. His love for me has driven me to return His love to Him. How can one return God's love? Give more money to charity or the church? Feed more homeless people? Go to church? Do more work at the local shelter? No! Jesus gives this answer, too.

"He who has My commandments and keeps them is the one

who loves Me; and he who loves Me will be loved by My Father, and I will love him and will disclose Myself to him." (John 14:21)

Loving God is not what you do for Him. If so, God could say, "What did I ever do before you were born and what will I do after you die?" There is nothing you can do that God needs. It is simply a matter of love. He loves you and He wants you to love Him back. When we love God, He has mysterious ways of rewarding us and blessing us.

CAN YOU IMAGINE TOTAL LOVE FROM GOD THE CREATOR, GOD THE GIVER AND SUSTAINER OF LIFE?

My first heart, given by God required only one thing. Someone had to die for me to live. The Son of God, Jesus, Immanuel (meaning God is with us), Prince of Peace, King of Kings, Lord of lords had to die for me to live. There has literally been no one else who could or would do this for me or probably you. But Jesus was willing to die for those who would call Him Lord.

Jesus' death and my acceptance brought me a totally new life. It wasn't void of trials and tribulations. Karen and I had difficulties with our marital relationship, raising our children, and like others, our finances, employment and health. Too many "false believers and preachers" will tell an individual if they will accept Jesus, as their Lord and Savior, He will do away with all their problems. I can neither find this truth in the Scriptures nor any serious believer I have known. One thing Jesus promises to do is walk <u>with</u> us through our troubles. The emphasis is on the "with".

On the other hand, I have found that some issues in life, the Father allows us to go through these trials and tribulations to allow us see Him at work in and through our lives. Going through the problems often reveal our character and the truth about our lives. We can learn from these encounters and avoid them in the future as well as see God work them out.

Servants who know how to take off their shoes and walk in humility before God can be used of God to walk in power. Like Moses on Mt. Sinai, the Mountain of God, he had to take off his sandals because he walked on holy ground. Do you know why Moses had to remove His sandals? God made Moses feet, man made the sandals. This is a symbolism that God wants nothing between Himself and us. I have found that when I talk off my sandals and walk in humility before the Lord; I see and experience God's great power and His merciful provisions.

The power, the might and the love of the Heavenly Father can motivate a willing person into a child and servant of the Almighty. What a Father He is!

4 A NEW ENCOUNTER WITH GOD
AND A NEW LIFE

Looking back in time, our move to Center opened not only a new chapter in our lives, but a whole new book. As Karen and I grew in the Lord, we truly began to more deeply understand His Word. The Scriptures became alive. We found direct application to our lives. As we submitted to Him, we found life got sweeter and more precious, between the two of us, between Karen, I and our children. The real impact was between us, our God, His church and our brothers and sisters in Christ. A whole new light shone in our lives.

As we continued to pray, God began to involve us in His ministry to people. Ministry is always a sacrifice. It is always beyond your ability, your talents, or your gifts. Only the Lord God can enable one to do His work and prepare one to fulfill one's purpose.

Karen, Mark, the Pastor of the Christian Church and me participated in a project called, "Christmas in July." This was a local mission's endeavor to assist hurting, needy people in our community. The funds for these projects were received at a Community-Wide Thanksgiving service, which was held each year. In July following Thanksgiving workers would assemble to go to homes and work on projects like building ramps for wheel-chair bound people or repairing a leaky roof.

Our team went "across the tracks" if you know what I mean? This was a part of town where the African-American community lived. I have to confess I had never seen a community so divided by a racial barrier. In fact, rarely would Anglos venture into this part of town. They had a false sense of insecurity. However this was a section of town I traveled in and out of frequently during my high school years to pick up my parents' employees. I felt right at home in East Center.

As the four of us approached the house I remember so vividly looking around. Across the street there were two men guzzling beer. These two men remained close by on their porch while we worked. One of the men asked, "Whatcha doing?" One of the team responded, "Putting plumbing and a bathroom in the house for this lady.

The house was an older frame home in a state you might expect for an older country house of a widow. Her toilet was an outhouse 50 or so feet in back of the house. There was no indoor plumbing what-so-ever. She would go to a line at the street and get water to wash or bath.

Our job was to take the city line, which came out of the ground, connect to it and run water into the lady's home. We installed a sink and shower as well. I have never seen someone so appreciative as the lady. She deeply impacted my life and ministry.

The Father gave me an opportunity to begin a weekly nursing home ministry. We had a lady that played the piano and I led the singing. After the singing, I would preach. Funny, the first time I preached I took eight pages of notes. Mark went with me. After we left he asked, "Do you know how long you preached?" My response was, "It seemed like it was forever." He told me I had preached for about 15 minutes. Wow! All the notes I made for a short message was overkill. I deeply felt overwhelmed but as the weeks progressed, so did I.

A few people in the church had heard about the need for medical equipment in the Ukraine. A couple of men approached the county officials about purchasing the old medical equipment from the closed county hospital. The funds were raised and the equipment purchased.

The team acquired two shipping containers. Some people disassembled the equipment and others carefully packed the equipment. Within days of completion a local man who owned a trucking company hauled the containers to Houston to ship to the Ukraine.

I truly believed the Lord God used my early years to form my passions of service, unrestrained by skin color or status within the community. Later, while in seminary, it seems as if the Father used these events plus others to mold me into the servant He would use.

I learned that God does not call the prepared, He prepares the called.

Neither Karen, nor I felt worthy. In fact, we aren't. Only God the Father and His Son, Jesus is worthy.

"I call upon the LORD, who is worthy to be praised, And I am saved from my enemies. (2 Samuel 22:4, NASB)

"For great is the LORD, and greatly to be praised; He also is to be feared above all gods. For all the gods of the peoples are idols, But the LORD made the heavens." (1 Chronicles 16:25-26)

"Then I looked, and I heard the voice of many angels around the throne and the living creatures and the elders; and the number of them was myriads of myriads, and thousands of thousands, saying with a loud voice, 'Worthy is the Lamb that was slain to receive power and riches and wisdom and might and honor and glory and blessing.'" (Revelation 5:11-12)

We alone are not worthy of anything except the penalty of sin – death (Romans 6:23). When you hear someone say, "you deserve"

- run! Don't believe it! We never deserve any great blessings of the Lord – they are each a free gift, a piece of Him, an expression of His great love.

Even God's call into Christian service is a great expression of His love. The call isn't a sentence of pain and agony – it is a magnificent expression of His love to involve us in what He's doing. God's call upon a person's life for ministry enables the person to personally experience what the Lord, God is doing. The participant is able to see people responding to the supernatural power of God.

When Jesus called the disciples, they had no idea what they were up against, trials and tribulations, surprises and blessing. Each disciple would see the Almighty at work through Jesus and slowly experience God. We did! One cannot expect to experience the full person of God at one time, for He is so complex that He will never be fully understood or known.

Jesus' death, burial and resurrection brought me a new life. It wasn't void of trials and tribulations. Karen and I continued with the normal struggles of family, finances and health. Too many "false believers and preachers" will tell individuals if they would accept Jesus as the Lord and Savior that He will do away with all their problems. Some will even espouse the ideal the reason why Christians suffer is because they do not have enough faith. I can neither find this in Scriptures nor have I found it in life despite an intimate walk with Christ

People are people. Everyone has struggles. Some are self-imposed and others have it thrust upon them. Life is full of unexpected occurrences and struggles. Disease still strikes the faithful in Christ. The faithful still die. We all still have to interact with others who may or may not walk in Christ.

On the other hand, I have found that some issues in life are through no fault of our own. The Heavenly Father allows us to go through these trials to allow us to see Him at work in and through our lives. Going through problems often reveals our true character and the dependent walk we have with our Savior. We can certainly learn from these encounters and if we are observant and teachable, we will see them as a course correction for our lives.

While wrestling with God's call upon my life was a time of many emotions flooding my heart and mind. This was also a time when I sensed the Lord making major adjustments in my life. He had to mold my character through experiences and learning like a sponge soaking up water. What was to come and did come was an extreme make-over. I asked myself repeatedly,

- o How could God call a person, like me, with my past, my sin and my weaknesses?
- o How could God call someone, like me, who did not know well the Scriptures?

I did not realize until later that it wasn't about me, but all about Him. God, the Father, chooses whom He wishes. God, the Almighty prepares the called, sends the receptive, and uses the available.

Karen reminded me, "I didn't marry a preacher, I married a banker." As excited and humbled as I was, she was not negative, but seeking God's answers, too. She spoke with our Associate Pastor and he encouraged her to allow God to take care of the question of my call. He comforted and encouraged her by reinforcing the fact that if God has called me into the ministry, He would provide and nothing could stop that, but if He had not called me, there would be nothing I could do to make it possible. Later she told me this was one of the greatest helps, ever.

I have personally witnessed several men who felt called into ministry and their wives were not willing partners, at all. Often, the wife was combative, unparticipating, and full of anger. I personally have never seen this situation work out for Kingdom productivity for the called servant. Oh, sure, he or she might teach Bible study and do ministry within the community, but pastoring a church is not a possibility if the wife isn't sold out to the Lord and the direction for her husband as well. (You may have a different opinion, but this is the bottom line I've come to in my experiences.) If the wife truly wants to honor her husband, she must also take off her shoes and walk humbly before the Lord.

Our new encounters with the Lord, gave us a completely new perspective and new life. Our old life was truly gone and we were living a new life – one with an unwritten script, one only to be written by God, Himself. Looking back, now – WHAT A FUTURE IT HAS BEEN! WHAT A FUTURE I AM STILL WAITING FOR!

I have discovered through personal Scripture study and prayer that God calls every redeemed person to His service. Not all serve in the same way, to the same extent or the same place, but still, He does not exempt anyone from serving Him. That's why we are redeemed (saved, born-again) in the first place. Some mistakenly think God saves us because He loves us and wants to spend time with us. Would you want to spend time with someone like you, before redemption?

No, we are redeemed to serve. God's love is there, but out of His love He saves us and calls us to walk along side of Him. Our walk with the Heavenly Father should be like two extremely close friends or very close siblings or even a married couple walking down a path or along a surf side. We walk together with God in the lead and we're along to follow Him. Nothing infuriates me more than to see the bumper sticker, "God is my co-pilot."

If God is your copilot – you are in the wrong seat. Through the years I have learned to release control. It has not always been easy for a Type A personality. Yet as the waves of trouble beat against the shore of our lives, I have gently and eventually realized, "I have never been in control in the first place." God knew it, but I had to figure it out. When I did discover this truth, life got a whole lot more peaceful. I found the temptation to worry or plans would arise and God would gently remind me, "I Am is in control".

5 NEW ENCOUNTERS REHABILITATES
NEW HEARTS

If you've ever known someone that has had a heart attack or any type of surgery, you will remember they had to go through rehab. One may have to go through rehab after a stroke, knee or hip surgery or a heart attack. I have found this time valuable for regaining strength and vitality under supervision. As I write this now, I am in cardiac rehab.

For one to be able to fully function, one has to be healthy and strong. After a cardiovascular incident, one "ain't" strong. After one has made a profession of faith in Christ, one is not strong, either. Oh, I'm sure there are self-righteous people out there that will say different. But, there are several things God has put into motion to strengthen the newly redeemed.

One is discipleship. Rarely are churches, these days, discipling people, so preparing people for ministry is hit and miss at best. Secondly, time is necessary to follow Jesus, learn from other mature believers and third, one needs ministry experience. All three can prepare a person for ministry, if one is willing. I don't say this because it is how God worked in our lives, but I see this throughout Scriptures as well.

One day in our Bible Study class my Old Testament professor asked, "How do you know you are where God wants you? This should be a question we continually ask ourselves over and over.

Are you where God wants you to be or have you excluded yourself from His great presence and blessings by walking away from Him?

I, personally, experienced more of God while in seminary than I have in all of the churches I have served combined. I find this sad, too! Seminary is a place of training, not God's house. But, I also understand the church isn't the white wooden or brick structure, it is the people, so in truth the seminary staff, faculty and students did make up a church.

There were many events at seminary where I saw the hand of God at work. God's work in my life further developed the new heart Jesus gave me over ten years earlier at redemption. I am not speaking of the numbers of professions of faith and baptisms. I speak of what, to me, is the genuine hand of God at work in my life and those around us. We experienced a Christ-like love and concern rarely expressed by folks in the pew.

After completing my undergraduate work Karen asked, "Now what?" I felt led by the Lord to give her this answer, "The Father went to a lot of trouble to get us to New Orleans, it seems like it would be a waste and a shame not to go on in theological education." Immediately I enrolled in the Master's program. Again, Karen asked, "What will you study?" This time I had no definite answer.

The three years of "new heart rehabilitation" in seminary was priceless. Students, in addition to their own churches, also had classroom experiences and chapel. Classroom time was extraordinary. The students had the best prayer time I've experienced anywhere. Chapel had the greatest minds and hearts of Christ proclaiming God's Word. The cafeteria had red beans, sausage and rice directly from heaven every Monday for lunch. Boy, were they good.

The Lord opened opportunities for the students to learn evangelism and ministry. Both were done on campus, but more especially off campus. We lived in Sodom and Gomorrah 70126 – that's New Orleans! There was a heavy conviction on campus about doing personal ministry and evangelism. Students, in addition to serving their church field, would go throughout the surrounding areas proclaiming Christ.

There was one exception. There were a few families, like the ones in our churches, that would never leave campus. New Orleans was too wicked. One student told me they never went to eat where they served alcohol. I asked him how his family liked McDonalds. Really? No alcohol in New Orleans? Just because a place has booze, doesn't mean one has to drink it!

The point I'm making is it appears that not all receive a new Christ-like heart. Whether we are in seminaries or in churches, we often see people that try to live their lives as though they are straddling a barbed-wire fence. One leg in one pasture and the other leg in the pasture across the fence, but never committed to either side.

The new heart Jesus gives builds boldness, strength, and confidence in the fact the He will provide and protect. Throughout our seminary days we were filled with plenty of experiences in our lives and others that God cares for His children and provides for the needs.

When most of us left seminary, we were willing to charge Hades with a water pistol. Later we would all discover independently that we weren't as powerful as we thought. Only God is powerful and we derive our power from Him.

After leaving seminary we faced the real world. I found people not as Christ-centered, excited and full of the Holy Spirit, as I either thought or hoped. Life suddenly became a lesson in human reality. I began to understand that the lives of the people within our churches are not always spirit-filled, redeemed, excited, or filled with praise – many times they simply existed in their momma's "religion".

You may think I'm judgmental? No, just observant! You see God called me within the ministry of evangelism, like the Apostle Paul. My ministry has been to go into churches and strengthen them by giving them the unadulterated Word of God, to preach the Word in season or out, and never, never tickle any ear. The phrase tickle any ear refers to the Apostle Paul's message to Timothy not to preach to the entertainment of the people of the church but to address the serious needs of their spiritual life as revealed by the Holy Spirit. (2 Timothy 4:3)

People misuse the word "judgmental" so often. It does not mean form an opinion, but to condemn. The Word of God tells us we should have a discerning spirit to tell the difference between the genuine and the fake. A discerning spirit can be a burden because you can see and sense the truth in situations and people that most do not have. But in order to direct lives from "self" to God, one has to be able to independently discern the truth because people will always let you see their best side and hide their darker side.

As you may guess, church work can be and many times is stressful, but fulfilling. One may see a lot of hurting within churches, but what a place to hurt! Hurting people can find the love of God, the hand of fellowship and the warm heart of a loving brother.

Ministers experience stress on many levels. There are the struggles of time conflicts where you need to be with your family, you need to spend time in your personal walk before God, administration of the church, preparing for Bible study and sermon delivery. In addition to these struggles there is the call and compassion for people and ministering to the deep needs of the people when there is a death in their family or life-threatening illness. Then there are those who just want to fight their Pastor and especially God. So a minister has the weight of his own family, the church and the needs of others in which to struggle.

I must confess my naivety. Truly, I thought people inside the church hungered and thirsts for righteousness as much as I did and they would be as excited as I was (still am) about ministering to the lost and the redeemed.

Don't we all expect a higher standard in those who say they follow Jesus? However, I noticed a much different response than I expected. As I said earlier, "people are people". Some walk in the Spirit, other walk in the flesh. Some are mature in their faith and others seem as if they've never experienced a "filling of the Holy Spirit" and these people wish to walk in their own understanding, wisdom and power.

I know you would not believe it, but people fight in a church. This presents a different stress level for the minister because these DEFCON (military term for Defense Condition) can change without signs or warning. Let me give you a true story I heard from another Pastor.

I had spent the morning in prayer preparing to preach God's Word. My heart and mind was totally centered upon the awesome responsibilities before me. As I walked from my office to the worship center a lady zinged me with this statement: 'Pastor, Pastor (with the emphasis of a life-threatening and eminent danger on the horizon) the ladies' restroom is out of toilet paper. What are you going to do?'

As he told this story he revealed how surprised he was and he was almost speechless because of his total spiritual mindset at that moment and he respond, "I'll pray for you!" At that moment he continued to walk to the worship center.

I am embarrassed to tell you of all of the personal attacks I have experience throughout the years. This is not uncommon among ministers, but we have to learn to determine what a genuine concern is and what is either from the flesh or the devil.

The new heart of the servant has to be willing to also hurt. One hurts for the people living in bondage. The heart is filled with pain for those living in bondage to Satan, whether in or out of the church. But God gives the heart to the servant for His service and to have a heart filled with compassion.

As I have talked with other ministers they tell of similar experiences and struggles. My first response is, "phew, I thought it was just me!"

Karen asked me once, "Do you think all the stress and wars within churches have caused your heart trouble?" I truthfully did not understand how to answer her. I remember telling her that this problem was inherited from my maternal grand-dad through my mother to me. At the point of this writing, I truly do not believe it was my work within the church. But this I feel with concrete conviction, the situation was used by God to glorify Himself. Countless times I should have dropped dead. In fact one doctor told Karen I would not live. More later.

6 LIFE IN THE TURMOIL

Let me skip a decade. The heart I inherited through my maternal grandfather was an opportunity for the Lord's work in my life. From 1988 to 2007, the doctors treated a total of eight heart-attacks. There were two by-pass surgeries, one in July 1996 and the second in December, 2007. The cardiologist implanted an ICD (inter-cardiac device or pacemaker and defibulator) in December 2010.

My heart attacks seemed to occur about every 2 to 4 years apart. The first one was in 1988 and the last one occurred in 2007.

Several have asked if these problems were due to lifestyle. No, these issues were due to genetics. Every cardiologist confirmed this fact. I asked my primary cardiologist one day, "You have mapped every artery and vein in my body from my neck to my ankles and have found everything completely clear, yet the arteries in my heart continue to plug and create a heart attack. Isn't that unusual? If my heart arteries continue to clog, shouldn't the rest of my circulatory system show similar signs?"

This was Dr. B.'s response, "Yes normally if the heart arteries are clogged, then the rest of the body will show similar problems. Your problem is due to a genetic heart problem you inherited from your mother."

Karen asked one cardiologist what could be done to stop these heart attacks. She was told, "Nothing! Everything we do now is a bridge until technology and medicines can be developed." We were also told just prior to transplant that medical technology makes major in-roads of discovery about every ten years and at this time (2015) there is nothing except transplant or to have a heart pump installed.

In 1996, While studying for a seminary final in the Old Testament book of Joshua a tremendous pain developed in my chest as an indication of the 1996 heart attack with an ensuing by-pass surgery. I had learned I test best when I get up early in the morning, about two o'clock and study hard before the final. That morning was no different except about 6:30 in the morning I told Karen, "I think it's happening again!"

She called an ambulance and they made their dramatic entrance on the quiet campus. We were off to the E.R with Karen and the kids following closely in the car.

When the ambulance arrived the EMTs wheeled me out to their vehicle and I remember weeping and saying to myself, "I don't have time for this!" Quietly in my mind I remember asking God, "Why did You allow this?" What am I going to do about my final in Joshua? Graduation is dependent upon completing this last class."

Karen called the seminary and talked with my professor and he told her to have me call him on the other side of this situation and he would make it up.

That was only the beginning of the things that happened that glorified our Heavenly Father. First, Karen later told me, after surgery, that the waiting room was filled with seminary students and professors praying for me. What a humbling moment I had when she told me this. I couldn't believe that many people would come on a school day and spend it in a waiting room.

Secondly, on the morning after my third post-operative day, the surgeon came into my room. One never knows what one will hear from their surgeon after surgery. He said, "You can go home!" Wow! Going home three days post-operatively was a treat and unusual.

I truly could not comprehend all of this, but to say I experienced a state of complete awe is an understatement. The first quadruple by-pass was done. Recovery took about three months to get stronger, but within three weeks of surgery I was living and pastoring in rural Central Mississippi.

I had been talking with my first post-seminary church and they called to see how I was doing. They told me when I was ready, to give them a call, and they'd come to New Orleans and move me.

In March 2004 God brought us back Texas to a church in Pasadena. I felt led by the Lord to go to this church. I knew they needed revitalization, which is the ministry in which God placed me. The Houston area was not on my list of favorite places to move. My opposition did not have anything to do with the church, only the location. I told Karen, "I haven't left anything in Houston, I haven't lost anything in Houston and I have never wanted to live in Houston. But I remembered Jonah. He didn't want to go where God wanted him to go, either; he resisted and look at what God did.

God revealed so much about the Pasadena church. He revealed it to me and many other mature, spirit-filled believers about the condition of this church. People were growing spiritually. We had instituted a disciple-making plan and there was a great excitement growing within the church. People were connecting to each other and they were getting excited about ministry opportunities to the community. Then war broke out.

A small handful of people begin to complain about the direction of the church. The church was in an older part of Pasadena and surrounded by Hispanics. In fact the demographics of that time indicated 70% of the neighborhood was Hispanic. Our discussions were about how to minister to our neighborhoods seemingly launched restlessness in this older group, who others told me had tried to control the church for the past 20 years. It was during this time I suffered my 5th heart attack.

About forty people, including Karen and I, left this church. Over the next few weeks several of those that left presented us with a new opportunity – start a new church. This was an exciting time because those who came were those more mature, spirit-filled people hungry to grow spiritually and minister to their community. We were able to hold Vacation Bible School in a large city park and minister to people in a moderate sized apartment complex. God led us to minister to a group of men in a drug and alcohol rehab center and love on them.

December, 2007 the next heart attack occurred and a second by-pass surgery. This occurred at home and the surgery was done at a local hospital in Pasadena Texas a few days before Christmas 2007. The surgery was done so quickly that neither Karen nor I had much of an opportunity to gather questions in our minds for the doctors. The second by-pass surgery was tougher, in many ways, than transplant surgery because there were so many unknowns. In transplant there were dozens of conversations and discussions before surgery. We had ten months to think, prepare and ask questions. We knew just about everything to expect.

The 2007 by-pass surgery, the second by-pass surgery was done on the morning of Christmas Eve. Our church gathered in the Chapel on the 23rd and we had our Christmas service and prayer. The next morning I would face the nervous time of facing the knife again.

The second surgery went well. Karen told me the following details after getting home. The morning of Christmas the pulmonologist came out and told Karen, "You know he is not going to live!" She said she told the doctor, "Merry Christmas to you, too! You just don't know him, do you?" Three years later I saw this same physician walking through the hospital. I walked up to him and explained who I was and told him this, "I just wanted you to know that I lived!"

Karen told me that the doctors had me in a medically induced coma for seven days. While in this comma a male nurse stayed at my bedside constantly guarding me like I was a prisoner in maximum security prison or that I was his brother, taking every measure for my comfort and recovery.

One night after the doctors began bringing me out of the comma they gave me a medication to help me sleep. Have you ever had a hallucination? They can seem so real even though it is your mind playing tricks. I saw myself chained to a cold, wet, dark stone wall in a prison cell. I called the nurse and demanded, "I haven't done anything. Let me out of this prison!" She tried comforting me, but I've learned sometimes a person has to stand firm and demand action. I made another demand to be released from prison and she refused. So, I did the next best thing and told her (not asked) to call my wife. The nurse said, "I don't have a phone." I remember telling her that wasn't my problem. I told her, "Get a phone or send smoke signals but get ahold of my wife!" She did and Karen came to the ICU rubbed my head and said, "Go back asleep" And I did. I had another event, but it wasn't too bad.

There were times I wondered what God was doing? Have you ever felt abandoned by God? There were short instances in which I wondered. How could God allow me to suffer and come so near death?

I remembered a biblical truth; God's faithfulness is not determined by Him always protecting us, always blessing us, or always allowing us to walk on the mountaintops. There are the valleys we have to walk through, mine were cardiac.

I discovered in suffering and or in pain, God can be appreciated, worshipped, and glorified. I keenly remember sitting in my ICU bed in Tampa, Florida the morning after being admitted with a heart attack. This was number three. Heart attacks, like any disease, can cause a person to do some serious soul searching. A quiet environment in ICU, if there is such a thing, can be very reflective, especially if you don't begin with an "oh me" attitude.

Feeling sorry for one's self is defeat that has already occurred. If you're feeling sorry about yourself, and who doesn't from time to time, you have accepted defeat! For me, I found when I begin an episode of "oh me" is a time I begin to focus on the life and blessings God has given me I have often sang the hymn, "Count Your Blessings"

When upon life's billows you are tempest tossed,

When you are discouraged thinking all is lost,

Count your many blessings name them one by one,

And it will surprise you what the Lord hath done.

The Psalms have also been a great help to me. King David, the writer of many, was a man of deep sorrows. He had people chasing after him, to kill him, as well as a man he deceptively caused to die in order to marry his wife. But David sought the forgiveness of the Lord and found restoration and peace.

Sometimes reading about the sorrows of other people and seeing how the Lord has answered them can help us through present troubles. There are plenty of examples in the past century of great people living in the midst of trials and tribulations.

Life has a natural way of getting in the way. Anyone that says they have not experienced turmoil is lying. Turmoil or tribulation for the follower of Christ is as natural as breathing. While I do not believe God brings this turmoil or tribulation upon His children, I do believe He allows it. Take Job, for example. We are told in Scriptures that Job was a righteous man. One day Satan came to God and accused God of taking extra special care of Job and Job's faithfulness was due to God's provisions and blessings. Satan challenged God to strike Job and watch Job fall like a rock. God told Satan he could test Job, but you cannot take his life.

Just because you are going through stuff, does not mean that God has forsaken you. It may mean several things: You may be suffering from the choice of lifestyle that you chose. Take for example a person who has smoked or drank heavily and they have bad lungs and or heart. You are suffering at your own hand, not Gods. You may be suffering because of the actions or words of someone else. Or, you may be suffering the normal disease process of hereditary or age. God is not under obligation to heal you, no matter what some "super religious" person may tell you or what you believe. But, the Father may use these situations to build your trust in Him and your faith.

> "but we also rejoice in our sufferings, because we know that suffering produces perseverance; [4] perseverance, character; and character, hope. [5] And hope does not disappoint us, because God has poured out his love into our hearts by the Holy Spirit, whom he has given us. [6] You see, at just the right time, when we were still powerless, Christ died for the ungodly. [7] Very rarely will anyone die for a righteous man, though for a good man someone might possibly dare to die. [8] But God demonstrates his own love for us in this: While we were still sinners, Christ died for us. [9] Since we have now been justified by his blood, how much more shall we be saved from God's wrath through him! (Romans 5:3-9, NIV)

Faith is built through the hammer of our tribulations. How do you come to rely upon something? Day-by-day you use it or experience it. God gave me a one-year old truck fifteen years ago. Day by day I have driven the truck, hauled stuff, pulled loads, and enjoyed it. When I climb into the seat and stick the key into the ignition, I am sure it will crank. Why? Because it has year after year, mile after mile, in cold weather and hot. Now, if you had a vehicle that would not crank more than it cranked, what would you do? Sell it!

This is not the best example, but let me go a different direction. How do you know God cares for you? Because God has said He cares in His Word. That's one reason, but the real reason is you can have a track record with God providing.

In the fall of 2009, I sensed God giving us a new direction, which would require faith and be a challenge. Karen had worked on her Bachelor's Degree in teaching for several years. She did not lack much. Since my cardiac life was so uncertain, we both made a commitment for her to return to school fulltime and complete her primary education degree. I felt that there might be a day either she or we would have to depend upon teacher's pay.

This was a financially difficult time. Karen's commitment resulted in a short tenure at the University of Houston – Clear Lake. However, God honored the commitment. She graduated in December, 2012. She was able to pass her state board exams quickly and worked as a certified substitute in the spring, 2013. This relieved the financial tension we had suffered for two years.

By May 2013, the principal of the school asked Karen if she would like to work there. The principal told Karen she'd get back to her in a couple of weeks because she had others to interview. Later that afternoon, the principal called and gave the job to Karen. She was going to teach Second Grade.

God has finished and provided within this time. He had allowed us to save money and use it during this time of monetary shortfall. He also provided for the future. Karen would now have a retirement and God would use this later in the post-transplant time.

7 LONG PREPARATIONS FOR
MY SECOND NEW HEART

The Uncertainty of the journey and The New Beginning of a New life

When I state "long preparations" I mean seven years. During the second by-pass surgery, I remember hearing a doctor say, "He has Congestive Heart Failure".

No doctor talked about it or discussed it with me. I continued my relationship with my primary care physician. Checkups would occur about every six months. Over the next two years, I mentioned to my primary care physician, that I remember hearing the term, "Congestive Heart Failure".

As the doctor searched through the thick medical records file he said that the cardiologist notes did not mention it, but there was one way to find out. He performed an echo-cardiogram, which was similar to the ultrasound Karen had done while she was pregnant with Lauren, our youngest. I asked the technician if she saw a boy or a girl. Talking about confused! I had to explain my humor.

My doctor walked back into the exam room looking as if he had seen a ghost. He told me my heart function was between 15 and 20 percent and I needed to go immediately to the cardiologist.

Immediately my primary care physician, Dr. B. referred me a young and highly skilled cardiologist. He would later be the cardiologist that referred me to the Center for Advance Heart Failure at Memorial Hermann, Houston (Texas Medical Center).

Dr. B. repeated the echo-cardiogram and confirmed what the previous doctor told me. He told me he would keep a close watch on the heart, the vital signs and my progress. Office visits for the next two years would be quite often.

As time passed I noticed physical strength and endurance was diminishing. I continued pastoring and substitute teaching and this presented no problem. The cardiologist gave me a new routine of monitoring diet, blood pressure and observing my legs for swelling was a routine that after transplant would be a way of life.

I knew like many diseases, heart disease is progressive. Once one has it, the doctors may be able to slow it down temporarily, but never stop it. One has to live with heart disease and make the best of it.

I offer the following details to illustrate how up and down the time waiting for transplant can be. There are so many variables that are not there with any other heart procedure that I wanted you to know of my struggles and how Jesus got me through this time.

I mentioned earlier that Mark, a fellow Pastor, a friend, a brother, a sojourner in the Lord and a man who mentored me early in ministry suggested I keep a journal of the events. I am glad I did. As I laid or sat in my ICU room, this exercise forced me to record my weaknesses and the Lord's strength and provisions.

The following dates and events are unedited. They are recorded as they came, day by day, or hour by hour. I have recorded what I heard, what I was told, what I felt, my frustrations, my brokenness, and God's intervention.

One of the focuses of my life has been this: God's given me this life, and I gave Him my life, so whatever He does, is His business. In the meantime, I refuse to surrender to my situation. I may be temporarily detoured, but until He takes me out, I am there to serve His needs and the needs of His Kingdom.

So, the following pages are straight from the computer diary I kept at home and in the hospital. The pages of the diary following surgery are entries made by either Karen, my wife or emails send by my closest brothers and sister that love me very much.

Let me repeat something I've said to many, doctors, nurses, social workers, transplant coordinators, my family and my friends and it is the truth

There has only been one Person to die for me, His name is Jesus, in dying He gave me the greatest gift ever – a new heart – His.

The benefactor of this earthly heart had to die, too to give me this heart.

Both died for the gift of my two new hearts, only one lives today – Jesus

The diary reads as follows from early 2014 through present day: This is provided so the reader might see the reality of the daily struggles of life and God's provisions.

<u>2014</u>

I offer you the following with the only motive to show you how God works. He works in His time and His way, but He does provide for His children whom He loves very much.

February 25th During Dr. B.'s office visit he began to discuss my need for cardiac intervention, either a heart pump or transplant. While this type of news is normal for a cardiologist, but not every patient hears this news.

May 13th Dr. B. mentioned that I was doing well, but the inevitable intervention would have to occur. He said he thought twenty years longevity was a stretch.

August 12th Dr. B. gave me a folder and a DVD on a heart pump. He thought this might be the most viable choice until transplant could occur. This idea troubled me deeply. The idea of having a mechanical pump with an external battery created a troubled spirit.

August 19th I had a follow up consultation with Dr. B. He answered questions. I began to accept that the pump might be my only option. I poured out my heart before the Lord somewhat searching, somewhat in a depression. I asked the Lord to consider a complete healing to glorify Him realizing this prayer was self-serving. He gave me Dr. L.'s name and phone at the Center for Advanced Heart Failure.

Dr. B. told me that cardiac care would be passed to Dr. L. and they would be able to discover where I am in heart health and the best course of action with a timeline. Dr. B. told me Dr. L. would be the next step to heart transplant.

This was a sobering moment. The realization that either my life would be over soon or God would have to intervene caused me think about myself for a change.

August 26th First meeting at the Center for Advance Heart Failure. Karen and I met Dr. L, and his colleagues. He was highly personable, showed deep compassion and was reassuring. He said they would perform a heart and lung test that would identify my heart's condition, treatment and a timeline for possible transplant. I continued seeking God for strength, courage and direction – too many questions.

Sept. 9th Went with Karen to heart and lung test. It was tough! Afterwards, Dr. L. discussed the outcome of the test and told me my heart was at a place that I am qualified for and desperately need a heart transplant. He discussed that he preferred transplant to pump – less problems and issues.

The transplant specialist came in to discuss all the protocols that would have to be met to be put on the list: CT scans, colonoscopy, dental, blood, heart catheterization, and meetings.

This put me and Karen in a deep mood of overload with a sense of "crises of belief". Neither of us talked on the way home. I went to bed at 8:30 pm to download the information in my own mind and fall asleep as soon as possible.

We both experienced deep, soul-searching and mixed emotions. On one hand finality was close by in the future but on the other hand, perhaps a solution to the long problem.

September 10th I called and talked to Randy. I needed a friend and brother to talk to and God used this call to give me strength and courage to face that which I will face. Karen and I talked tonight, seemed as if we had worked through our concerns and began to make arrangements, a mental list of things to do and how we can pull the entire family into the arrangements to take the load off of us.

September 11th I Went to School District office to get my substitute ID and sign on code for work. Got home and Carina called from the Center for Advanced Hear Failure to make appointments for the pre-surgical protocol test. After talking with Karen, we agreed on test for September 17th and counseling, testing on the 25th, and angiogram on the 26th. We talked with Sean and Lauren about getting together Sunday night for the family plan of action. Talked to Blue Cross / Blue Shield and found a blessing of a maximum out of pocket expense of $6,300. I initially thought we would have to pay out $150,000. I cried out, "HALLELUJAH!"

The pre-surgical testing schedule is all arranged. The details and testing are extensive. The agenda is mind-boggling. However, the finances seem to be in order and we are off to transplant. Appointment made for final dental work next Monday. The Lord has worked out a lot of details. As Freddie prayed today, "Lord, please work out the details to Your glory." Now, the Lord has to work out all of the details of testing and counseling in order to get my name on the transplant list.

September 12th Received news today that my $5,000 deductible is presenting a roadblock. The sleep study and the colonoscopy will be an out of pocket expense. Sleep lab at Memorial Hermann is $4000. Money we do not have. I called and cancelled appointments for sleep, colonoscopy and protocol testing– indefinitely. Unless the Lord provides, these will not be done. I called Brandi, my transplant coordinator and left a message about postponing the next procedures indefinitely. I called Karen and gave her the news.

About 4:15 I received a call from the head of finances of Memorial Hermann Hospital on his private cell, while he is on vacation. He pleaded with me not to postpone this process due to the importance and necessity. He made it plain that we did not need to bring the money to the procedures, but next week they would see what kind of options there might be, such as: sliding scale payment, a discount or grants. I agreed to go through this process as planned.

Karen told me last night that she believed this was a provision of the Lord and I have no choice but submit. The Lord has had His hand upon my life since salvation in a unique and marvelous way. I should have died 27 years ago. Instead, He has guided my life through the heart attacks, two open-heart surgeries and a pacemaker.

The pacemaker and defibulator was an interesting device. It was installed just under my skin on my left shoulder just under my collar bone. It had wires that went directly to the heart. The reason for its installation was that the heart was in such serious deterioration that it could go into spasms. Dr. B told me if the heart did go into spasms, I would only have seconds before the heart failed. The device would pace my heart if necessary and shock if it went in uncontrolled high level of beats.

There was a small box next to our bed hooked up to a phone line. Every Monday morning about 2 a.m., it would read the results of the heart for the past week and send a report to the monitoring company. If there was a problem they'd contact the cardiologist. In early April, 2015 the device reported a short 2 second episode and that's what got me hospitalized on April 23, 2015 to ICU for more immediate transplant.

September 13th This morning was a time before the Lord. I still stand in complete amazement of the what the Lord has and is doing. The Holy Spirit reminded me of what the Lord told Moses to tell the people, "Do not fear! Stand by and see the salvation of the LORD which He will accomplish for you today."

The Lord is fulfilling this in my life, now. I sat this morning weeping while praying to the Lord. I previously committed my life and voice to proclaim His great mercies and redemption. Is it possible God is preparing to use me in my senior years?

September 16th Lauren has blossomed with an outpouring of love and work. She has posted the financial need to "Gofundme" with a $25,000 goal and as of today we've received $600. People we haven't seen in some time and people we do not know are responding. Larry said last night he was going to post it to his Facebook. Family and friends are responding. Karen got me a sub job at Atkinson next Wednesday

September 24th Hallelujah, the Lord is continuing to providing exceedingly beyond what I could have ever imagined!

September 26th The Lord is still providing – we received a prayer card from Nassau Bay Baptist Church. Linda and John donated $200 plus sent a $100 for travel, parking and food. I spoke with St. Luke's about sleep study. She asked about whether I've met deductible. I told her I had over $6k in test last week. She said they'd assumed the deductible had been met and to go ahead and they would allow me to do the sleep study on September 29th The colonoscopy cannot be scheduled until the week of October.

September 29th Sleep study performed. Nothing had changed with my CPAP settings.

October 9th Doctor's visit with Dr. O., endocrinologist to consult on the spot the CAT Scan found on my adrenal gland. He ordered several blood tests.

October 16th Dr. S.'s office visit (initial) resulted in the news my kidneys are weak, per blood and urine test and he wants to do other test to determine kidney function. Indications show acute kidney failure from the blood and urine test.

October 20th Brandi (Transplant coordinator) called and gave the results of Dr. O.'s blood test indicated no issues with the adrenal gland and he had released me for transplant.

This short time of 11 days presented an uncertainty that Karen and I had to pray through. We felt certain that there was no problem, but we will trust in the Lord.

October 24th Had a Kidney Echo test performed at Memorial Herman. The echo technician, Jimmy asked what I do and I told him I was a Pastor. He told me that his findings indicated there was plenty of blood supplied to the kidneys. Then we had a divine moment. Jimmy and I spoke about trusting the Lord God and devoting our lives to Him. He said he had been seeking answers we spoke about.

October 25th I received a letter from Dr. O.'s office. The Lord has provided a leap over the endocrine question of whether the spot on the left adrenal gland would present a problem for transplant.   He said the blood chemistry indicates the spot presents no problem. I had a renal echogram Friday and awaiting Dr. S.'s reply.   Dr. O. told me the elevated hematocrit and hemoglobin was the body needing to produce more red blood cells to compensate for a lower oxygen level, possibly due to sleep apnea. (Strangely enough Karen and I talked about that issue a few days ago and I mentioned to her that I believe the issue is due to diminished cardiac output.) I truly believe my elevated creatinine and BUN levels are from overmedicating and diminished cardiac output and I will either be put on the transplant list or the Lord will provide an ultimate healing without surgery.

The present situation requires I remain in Houston for transplant. This is quite possibly the reason why the Lord has caused us to remain here. However, might it be possible that the Father will completely heal me and then allow me to move on in His Kingdom's service?

November 11th In my monthly visit with Dr. L. he informed me I would need a kidney transplant, per Dr. S.'s blood test and visit. Brandi was compassionate and filled with grace and mercy. As I wept from the news, she was extremely pastoral and loving.

November 24th A kidney test was completed at Memorial Hermann to determine if my kidneys were damaged.

December 4th   Doctor's visit to Dr. S. resulted in the news that the test about kidney function showed results that no kidney transplant is needed. The results indicate kidneys are functioning at 51%. He said that the kidney function could stop after transplant and I'd have to go on dialysis. Isn't God truly at work removing road blocks?

December 16th We received news from Brandi that I was approved for heart transplant pending results from Hematologist for elevated hematocrit and hemoglobin.

December 17th Today was my follow up with Dr. H., gastroenterologist, for results of colonoscopy indicated 7 polyps and a diverticulum, but the pathology was negative for cancer. Due to follow-up in two years.

December 30th Email to Brandi that symptoms seem to be worsening: shortness of breath, appetite down, energy down and unable to walk any substantial distance.

2015

January 2nd Brandi called and asked me to be at Dr. L.'s office Monday (January 5, 2015) and they would determine what the next step would be.

January 5th Met with Dr. L. and said he wanted me to be at the catheterization lab Tuesday, (6th) for a right heart catheterization to see what the heart is doing. He told me depending upon the outcome of the test I would be admitted. (If the heart is continuing to go down would be the criteria).

January 6th Today was the heart catheterization. Registration informed me that my amount due was $6,350. However, since they were unable to process the claim in time to notify me, they would bill me. This is the maximum out-of-pocket annual expense.

My response was again a realization that the Lord was satisfying my annual out of pocket expense for 2015. The rest of the year should have no copay.

I heard Dr. L. commented in the catheterization lab, "We're going to admit him" A little while after returning to catheterization lab the nurse began an IV of a cardiac drug and said they were awaiting a room. Admitted to room 539 Heart Vascular Institute of Memorial Hermann in the Texas Medical Center.

This was an emotionally painful day for me on several levels. I did not want to be institutionalized. I felt a loss of freedom, mobility and ministry function.

January 7th Staff cardiologist came by and explained that the IV would run Wednesday through Thursday and they would re-catheterize to see if the heart has improved. He informed me if the heart has made satisfactory improvements, I would go home with the IV on a pump until transplant. If the heart has not improved they will admit me to ICU until transplant.

January 8th I had my bone marrow test and there was no discomfort at all! I should have the results in about 10 days. Initially, my nurse came in with tears in her eyes because she had heard that I was being transferred to ICU. We had just talked about my question of doubt whether I wanted to go that direction and live in ICU until transplant or not.

I called Sean and Lauren and asked them to be prepared for Karen to get the bad news. I called the school, asked for the principal and was told she was in a meeting. I told Ms. E. I needed to speak with Karen, but I would prefer that Karen not be in the classroom and asked if she could send someone in to relieve Karen and ask her to come to the phone. I told Karen I was going to ICU. I could tell she was contemplative, but she was more comforting to me than I was for her. She said, "We'll get through it!"

Dr. N. came by and said there was so little improvement that the next step should be to send me directly to ICU until transplant. He added that he cannot transfer me to ICU because I'm not on the transplant list yet and won't be until clearance from Hematology is received from the bone-marrow test. He gave me two alternatives:

1) To go home with the IV and chance it. The chances are at this point that I'd run into trouble,

2) Or, stay in the room, go through and increase IV therapy and retest Monday. I told Dr. N., I'd stay and see if it would help.

I am experiencing a huge "crises of belief". I am having an extreme dislike of living at 6411 Fannin (Memorial Herman – Texas Medical Center). I have told my entire cardio team of doctors. All previous hospitalizations for serious heart issues have been emergencies and did not require a lot of thought, just faith. This time, I have way too much time to think.

The Lord has led me to the word "remember", remember what He has already done. I preached this word last Sunday (January 4th) never realizing how important a word this would be for me the following week.

Despite everything, I have realized that the Lord was talking to me. It would require that "I" remember what the Lord has done. The Father's continued work in my health is widely thought to be that He still has something for me to do. My crisis of belief needs to be turned into faith. FAITH REQUIRES ACTION. I am to proclaim and have faith, I must respond to what God's doing.

God has never said, "Like it! He said, "Just trust Me!"

Reviewing what God has done:

1. Has taken me through the cardiac history,

2. The timely referral of Dr. B. to refer me to the Center for Advanced Heart Failure,

3. Discovering a deeply rewarding compassion and care from the center and hospital,

4. So far – There are no huge bills from the hospital or doctors,

5. Pre-transplant listing delayed due to additional testing,

6. Notification from Brandi (December 16th) approved for transplant pending maintaining basic metabolic index and outcome of hematology from the test on December 8^{th,}

7. No huge dollars needed for heart catheterization and bone marrow test the week of January 6th,

8. Doctors are telling me, submit or possibly die,

9. Visited with ICU staff Saturday night (January 10) while Karen and I walked. We felt comfortable talking and having our questions answered. Karen and I have discussed the fact that God has not brought us this point to abandon us. Yet, many questions still persist,

- If I don't work, I don't have insurance and if I don't have insurance, I can't have the surgery and if I don't have the surgery, - I DIE!,

- So far, God has provided, and He will provide now,

My faith in God requires my action. That is submit to what He is doing and trust Him for the outcome – finances, extended stay in ICU, income, and insurance .

January 12th Third heart catheterization performed by Dr. N. – results 2.27 which means passed and get to go home.

Dr. R. from oncology & hematology had no issues with hematocrit or hemoglobin. He said they were normal and the panel on the marrow was clear. So should be cleared for Dr. L.

A nurse came into insert PICC line. I was concerned about the pain, but there wasn't any pain except for the lidocaine stick. A PICC line is an IV they insert into the inner right arm between the elbow and the armpit. The line goes into the heart and delivers critical medications directly to the heart.

Pharmacy and home health came by to verify my information and give some details about the pump.

February 3rd Got an explanation of benefits from the insurance. My IV therapy cost for January 13-26 $28,500. Talking about blowing a cork! My portion is $1,200. This means a full month's IV therapy will be $65,769.23.

Obviously my initial "sticker price shock" took me by surprise. But, then the Father has been supplying funds through donations for my medical expenses. Up until my hospitalization of January 6, 2015, all bills are paid. I have no reason to believe the Father will slow down on or stop.

Larry, Lisa and Sara have devised a way to help with the transplant expenses. He's created a website to collect recipes. Our hopes are there will be many recipes that we can publish in a book and sell for $10.00 and take the profits for transplant expenses.

I pondered 1 Peter 1:3-9 "Blessed be the God and Father of our Lord Jesus Christ, who according to His great mercy has caused us to be born again to a living hope through the resurrection of Jesus Christ from the dead, to obtain an inheritance which is   imperishable and undefiled and will not fade away, reserved in   heaven for you, who are protected by the power of God through faith for a salvation ready to be revealed in the last time. In this you greatly rejoice, even though now for a little while, if necessary, you have been distressed by various trials, so that the proof of your faith, being more precious than gold which is perishable,   even though tested by fire, may be found to result in praise and glory and honor at the revelation of Jesus Christ; and though you have not seen Him, you love Him, and though you do not see Him now, but believe in Him, you greatly rejoice with joy inexpressible and full of glory, obtaining as the outcome of your faith the salvation of your souls."

And 2 Peter 1:5-8 "Now for this very reason also, applying all diligence, in your faith supply moral excellence, and in your moral excellence, knowledge, and in your knowledge, self-control, and in your self-control, perseverance, and in your perseverance, godliness, and in your godliness, brotherly kindness, and in your brotherly kindness, love. For if these qualities are yours and are increasing, they render you neither useless nor unfruitful in the true knowledge of our Lord Jesus Christ."

I believe some think I do not have faith or I feel sad. Quite the contrary! This ordeal has shaken me to the bedrock of my spirit. To think that Jesus is the only one who has died for me and in that death gave me a new heart. Now to know someone else will have to die for me to live. Many try to dismiss this in that the donor will be giving a special gift. Yes, but he will still have to die.

The level of weeping thanksgiving is enormous. To think – the Lord has kept me through these health issues for nearly 28 years. I have no doubt, what-so-ever; His hand has been upon my life. What's mind boggling is His degree of love and care for my life. My deepest hope is that He will be able to use this experience to glorify Himself, so that He might draw men and women to Himself.

I do have a concern – Karen! She's going through so much at work. They are stressing her out! On the surface she handling the transplant, but I cannot breach the depths of her heart to see what her struggles truly are.

March 13th I received a phone call from Sara at the transplant center. She told me that as of that day, insurance has approved the medical necessity for transplant and I have been listed on the national registry. She verified my contact phone numbers.

While I am on the bottom of the list, Dr. L. and all feel that transplant will happen very soon, any day, any week or within the next 2-3 months. My AB+ blood makes me a universal recipient, able to take any blood type, O, A, B, or AB. All have said this is to my advantage in getting a heart more quickly. I was told to keep my cell phone close at hand at all times because they never know when I will get a call.

I told Sara, "What a gift God has given me!" AB positive means this process can take place any time. In addition, I told her, in Jeremiah 29:11 God says, "I have known you since before I formed you in your mother's womb." Despite inheriting a genetically bad heart from my mother, and her from her father, God no doubt knew this day would come and gave me this wonderful and rare blood type. This caused me to weep in thanksgiving because of God's demonstration of His great love and compassion for me. To know that He knew this day would come before I was ever conceived – is awe filling.

Several have asked me, "Are you getting anxious?" Surprisingly, I am not. I felt the Holy Spirit giving me an explanation. When you know the facts and trust, anxiety is replaced with peace. I feel well educated on this subject (knowledge) because of all of the conversations that had taken place over the previous months and the gazillion questions asked by Karen and I to the transplant team.

The main knowledge is not what the transplant team has told me, but the revelation of my Heavenly Father of His outpouring of provisions throughout the past 27 and one-half years of heart attacks and surgeries. How the Father has orchestrated the past year is beyond my expectation or wildest imagination. How He has provided me with the ultimate in heart care from my cardiologist to the Center for Advance Heart Failure. The understanding that God gave me a way to go home from ICU with a continuous IV that has kept me alive and functioning showed He is in control. To see Him work out all the details, of finance, health, spiritual & mental well-being and the complete peace I have received from Him, alone.

His working in my life has given me the second part of the peace (lack of anxiety). TRUST   I have come to trust Him more and more as I go.   I feel like I am having my "burning bush experience", my own parting of the Red Sea. I do not know what tomorrow holds, but I know Who holds tomorrow in His hands and I am deeply humbled and thankful.

March 20th The nurse case worker from my insurance called. We talked about the whole process. Today she told me that I might have insurance coverage of travel expenses for hotel, meals, parking and etc.

March 23rd   I spoke with my insurance today and they confirmed that I have $10,000 in travel related transplant expenses reimbursement, including hotel, meals, mileage and parking. This is also an amazing provision I had never thought about. They will call me back with the details.

My next prayer thought is, "how will He provide for decreased income for whatever time I am off?"

April 9th   Karen's posting on Facebook

> "We got some exciting news this morning at the doctor's office. When we were admitted to the back waiting room, the transplant coordinator and the nurses were all asking us, "Have you seen the doctor?" "Has he told you?" We didn't know what was going on, then he walked by and said, "We came one inch away from calling you last night for our transplant!" While we were sleeping peacefully in our bed last night, the transplant team was talking about giving Billy a heart!

> It turns out that another patient at another hospital in the Medical City here had a greater need. Billy has AB+, so transplant is easier for him to receive. He can accept any blood type. We are encouraged and understanding even more the idea of what is about to happen! Please pray for this patient who received this gift of life today and please pray for the family of the one who has given. It truly is a beautiful sacrifice to give for someone else. We were told by the doctor's transplant coordinator that our gift could be very soon.

> I told Karen today this journey has been similar to Israel's journey from Egypt, through the desert on their way to the Promised Land. We have experienced the mighty hand of the Lord in ways that I could have never expected. The

Heavenly Father's provisions are beyond description, but His love is overpowering.   Live or die, I'm in His presence."

April 21st Dr. L. said today he wants to do another right heart catheterization and admit me to ICU for Swan line, new medication and elevation on the transplant list to "1A".

The "1A" list is the top priority of the transplant list.   Prior to admission my listing was "1B", which is a priority, but not the highest level.   Once a patient is listed on the National Transplant Registry, the priority becomes greater and more immediate in need.

April 23rd Heart catheterization completed late in the afternoon. They had no ICU room to move me into.   Finally about 5 pm, they moved me to room 820 with an unknown time table, perhaps until transplant.

May 2nd Nurses said supposed to be moved to transplant floor. About 9 p.m. the nurse said they actually did not have a room on the transplant unit – only IMCU 5.   So, no move for now.

May 3rd Dr. K.   the head of the transplant program at Memorial Hermann visited today – he said, "You almost got your heart last night. The man that received the heart had closer antibodies to the donor heart.   You are now number 2 on the list, but that could mean you are next."

May 6th The Executive Chef came by today and invited Karen and I to a specially prepared meal tomorrow evening.   What a blessing the Father has given to break the monotony.

Memorial Hermann Hospital takes excellent care of their "1A" patients.   We were known as "long-timers" or those who live at the hospital.   Many "1A" patients are fully functional, only restricted because of their diminished heart function and therefore have to be constantly monitored. So the hospital and staff goes more than the extra mile to make us feel comfortable and take our minds off of the life-threatening disease we have and to give us a glimpse of normalcy. Sometimes I would unplug my heart monitor to see if the nurses' hearts were working. They would come running in and I held the wire up so they could see it. They didn't think it was funny! But this was a way of keeping my sense of humor and a semblance of life and pass the enemy of the ticking clock of boredom and the threat of death.

One Sunday afternoon the nurses of the transplant unit provided an ice cream bar for the patients. They rolled a cart into each room and allowed us to pick all the ice cream and toppings we wanted. They wanted all the patients to know they were loved and as professionals they were more interested in the patients than just a chart, mediations, treatments and vital signs.

Despite the circumstances, I still see that our Heavenly Father provided me with a situation that I will remember the rest of my life. I learned a lesson many years ago with Karen birthing our children: with time one can forget the pain and discomfort and remember the blessings. Isn't that a truly merciful gift God has given us?

May 4th These days have been sort of difficult. I haven't seen Lauren or Sean in more than a week and have not seen Karen since last Sunday. Our phone conversations are very brief at 11:30 a.m. and she wants to talk about school and problem parents. I feel like I have been abandoned!

I am spending more time in the Word, praying and reading the book "gods at war" by Kyle Idleman about idolatry. The staff members of ICU are, in a small way, taking up the isolation and loneliness of family by being very warm and compassionate. They share a love that I have longed to see.

May 15th   I read in the Psalms this morning the following passage:

> "Those who know Your name trust in You because You have not abandoned those who seek You, LORD. (Psalm. 9:10) Lift me up from the gates of death, so that I may declare all Your praises." (13,14)

> "And He went into their synagogues throughout all Galilee, preaching and casting out the demons. And a leper came to Jesus, beseeching Him and falling on his knees before Him, and saying, 'If You are willing, You can make me clean.' Moved with compassion, Jesus stretched out His hand and touched him, and said to him, 'I am willing; be cleansed.' Immediately the leprosy left him and he was cleansed." (Mark 1:39-42)

I have long maintained a prayer parallel to Mark 1:39-42. The text previous spoke of how the healing miracles of Jesus drew attention to His power and compassion. I am continuing to pray, "Lord, if you are willing to completely heal this damaged heart, may it glorify You and draw attention to You.

I have been amazed at the attitudes of many people that, for some reason, do not believe God heals people today. Some nurses believe, others have a "faith" but believe it is modern medicine. MY OWN BELIEF IS – IT IS GOD AND ONLY GOD WHO CAN DO THE HEALING! MAY GOD BE GLORIFIED!

This transplant became a family affair. All members of the family, a gaggle of friends and many anonymous donors pitched in financially to help with the enormous expenses, emails of encouragement and most powerfully, prayers. There were people on bent knees praying across the U.S. and in Jamaica for God's intervention.

May 15th by Larry Jernigan

Here is my brother Bill Jernigan. He currently is the Heart Transplant unit at Herman Memorial Hospital in the Medical Center in Houston. He's been there ongoing three weeks. This may turn out to be a long haul project although he is on the A1 list. One patient this week was there for 365 days in the transplant unit before he received a new heart. His medical concoction you see in the photo is the keeping his heart going. It is being pumped directly into his heart by a heart an intravenous line.

Lauren posted this on Gofundme

Words fail me when trying to thank each and every one of you for all the support, both emotionally and financially, you have provided.

My dad is currently (as of mid-April) living in ICU awaiting transplant. The doctors are quite certain it will be ANY DAY! He has been moved up to position #2 on the waiting list.

Since he has been there, he heard through the grapevine that a heart almost went to him, but another patient with a greater need and better anti-body match had been identified. I loved to hear that he was in no way disheartened or frustrated by this. In fact, my parents told me they said a prayer, thanking God for providing for another when they needed it. Their turn will come soon to celebrate, and only when God knows they are truly ready.

For those of you wondering what one does when one do while waiting In ICU indefinitely, but is not "isolated" in the traditional sense one. Some of us were granted the privilege of occasionally walking the hallways occasional hallway walks when accompanied by a nurse. He has all of his favorite western movies on DVD, as well as Wi-Fi and Netflix. From what I've been able to tell, nothing entertains him as much as trying to crack a smile on some of the more severe doctors and nurses faces.

Please do us a favor, and visit . Larry and Lisa Jernigan (my dad's brother & sister-in-law) have worked tirelessly and selflessly to put together a world-class cookbook full of 300+ recipes donated by supporters from around the world. This is a great way to give a little, and get something in return to remember the journey for which we are over-joyed you have chosen to join us.

Talk to you soon! Lauren Jernigan Pelc

May 16th I asked the nurse this morning how many "1A's there were on the floor. She said two, including me.   Clearly the right heart for the right chest – God will have to provide. I know the Father has been teaching us to "wait upon Him".

The days are getting long and so are the nights. The hospital food is getting more tasteless. The doctors are saying my numbers look good. I am getting to walk whenever the nurses have time.

June 2nd This Thursday will mark the sixth week in ICU. The days are continuing to be long and lonely. The nurses and doctors are an interruption to an otherwise bland day.

I guess I am becoming depressed. Laughter hasn't completely escaped me and the nurses. The staff see me as a jolly fellow. One nurse from the other wing of 5th floor gave me a hug as I walk. Many of the nurses really try to make my day special.

Genevieve went to Dr. K. the other day and asked for an order not to disturb me between the hours of 10 p.m. and 4 a.m. For the two consecutive days prior my nurse would come into the room in the middle of the night, flip on a light and wake me up to do something they could have done earlier while I was awake. Since Genevieve and Dr. K. posted the note on my door, I've slept. I am grateful to the Lord for sleep. It is rest, but it also a way to pass time.

A note to show you how close we all became, Genevieve was never my nurse. All the nurses would care for other nurses patients and love on us.

Karen will be out of school this Friday, June 5th. I regret that her summer will be filled with either my absence or illness. I know we committed to each other, "in sickness or health" but I hate being away so alone, without her, Sean or Gizmo.

Karen told me Gizmo lost another tooth. My little one is aging like me. I can only hope the Lord will allow me to love on my little feller and see his tail wag as he greets me. "Gizmo is our 13 year old Pekinese.

I continue to ask the Father for His Divine hand to completely heal this broken, sick heart to His glory. Other day I read in Psalm 13

> "LORD, how long will You continually forget me? How long will You hide   Your face from me? How long will I store up anxious   concerns   within me, agony in my mind every day? How long will my   enemy dominate me? Consider me and answer, LORD, my God. Restore
> brightness to my eyes; otherwise, I will sleep in death, my enemy will say, "I have triumphed over him," and my foes will rejoice because I am shaken. But I have trusted in Your faithful love; my heart will rejoice in Your deliverance. I will

sing to the LORD because He has treated me generously."

I am trying to remain positive. I am 100% convinced the Lord can heal this heart without surgery or additional intervention. As I read in Mark chapter 5 this morning – a lady with a long history of blood illness touched the hem of Jesus' garment and was instantly healed. Jesus told her, 'Your faith has made you well. Go in peace and be free from your affliction.' Following that the synagogue leader came seeking Jesus' help for his dying daughter. People came and reported that the leader's daughter was dead. (Verse 35) In the following verses Jesus went to the home and raised her from the dead.

There are so many that refuse to believe or accept the Divine power of Jesus unto healing or resurrection. I must admit that I have not seen anything like Mark chapter 5, but I still believe that Jesus can heal this heart to His glory.

I would rejoice exceedingly if the Father would hear my prayer for healing, heal me and be glorified to the amazement of our nation. Our churches, our people, and our nation need a fresh awakening. I hope the lukewarm, the unbelieving and the skeptical still have an opportunity to see God, fear Him and discover His wonderful love for His creation.

I have discovered an error in my theology! God does not want to be "first" among many things in our lives. He wants to fill every space within our hearts, our minds, our thoughts, our actions and every aspect of our lives. We should be so filled with Him that there is no room, at all, within us for anything or anyone else.

June 4th Today began pretty much as any other day, except in the knowledge Karen would be coming this afternoon. Today was the last day of kids and tomorrow would be Karen's last day of work for the summer.

Megan, my nurse, came in around 2 p.m. to draw blood. She said it was for typing and cross-matching for the "1A" list. The nurse would not disclose the true reason for the blood draw because only the doctor could reveal the possibility whether this was of a transplant that day.

Dr. L. came in about 4:15 p.m. and told me they have a heart offer and I was one of three they were examining the antibodies for a match. He wanted to prepare me for the possibility that today would be transplant day.

I called Karen, Lauren, Larry and a member from our church, David to let them know we're awaiting the word, "go". Karen asked if I was excited. I remember throughout the night feeling absolutely nothing. I told her no, "We'll go if it's a go and not go if not."

Karen remained, I believe, on a heightened readiness. She wanted to stay as long throughout the night, just in case they came in to prepare me for transplant. She left at 11:30 p.m. and texted me as she progressed home so I would not worry about her.

Last night was slightly restless. I was tired, tried to go to sleep about 10 pm. Karen's alarm awakened me and so from 11:30 p.m. until 12:15 a.m. I stayed up. From 1:00 a.m. to 3:00 a.m. the IV alarms kept going off. So, I was awakened at 7:00 a.m. tired and still sleepy.

My thought last night was, if transplanted, God would not get as much glory as He healed me. But then, I remembered praying, "Not my will, but Yours!"

> "Then the angel said to me, 'Write: 'Blessed are those who are invited to the wedding supper of the Lamb!' And he added, These are the true words of God."(Revelation 19:9)

Baruch Haba shem Adonai – which in Hebrew means "blessed is He whom comes in the name of the Lord!"

June 7th Brandi, my transplant coordinator called at 12:15 a.m. with news they have me a heart. She stated it was a very good heart, located out of state, from a 15 to 25 year old. She did not have an operating room time.

She asked if I was excited, and I told her, not really. We were hoping for transplant for the first week of June because school was out last Friday.

I called Karen and she had some sort of doubt as to why I was playing a joke or was this real. Lyantie called and we prayed together. Lauren, Sean and Karen got here around 2:00 a.m.

So, June 7th will be my new birthday. It is the day the Lord has given me my second heart. The first heart was the most precious – the one Jesus gave me. This one will be special too. This marks the second person who had died to give me life. Jesus was the first.

7:00 a.m. Nurses coming on duty and getting off came by the room with expressions of thanksgiving for our time. We've all been together for 6 plus weeks and have come to appreciate and love each other.

1:30 pm – Dr. K. came to the room and asked if I had heard anything. He said they've called off surgery for the day because upon examination, the transplant team declined the heart upon visual examination due to heavy traumatic damage. The family (Mark, Lauren, Sean) were quiet. I believe the family was experiencing shock, disbelief and possibly hurt for me.

I can only say what I expressed to a lady in our church later in a text message, "Disappointment is an emotion when I am in charge, and peace is what one feels when God's in charge."

I could feel and sense disappoint in Dr. K.'s spirit. Yet, I did not feel remorse or disappointment – we all felt a peace.

Afterward, Lauren and Sean went to get Karen and I Mexican food. I ate as if I had not eaten in days. I was hungry and somewhat relieved that today was not the day of surgery. After lunch, we both laid down on the bed and slept for a couple of hours before Karen had to leave for home.

June 9th Lyantie, a close friend and sister in Christ, called and I lost all sense of time, but what a blessing. We talked about a lot of things, but I felt a deep, deep love for me as I have always felt from her. I told her about my identification with the prophet Jeremiah and that deep burning within my bones to see God Almighty glorified and honored by all people, but especially His "own".

I also mentioned to Lyantie that I really do not want a transplant, but would prefer to have a complete healing. I have confessed to the Father that I know I am slightly selfish, but He knows what is deep inside and my dream or vision is that He would choose a way that would gather the most glory for Himself. That He would take the impossible route (in the minds of people – healing) and show His churches, and the world that He is real and His care is real and His love is real and His calling of all humanity to His throne of worship is real.

We talked about tears of joy – those inexpressible words of worship and gratitude for being in the very presence of Almighty God and His Son, Jesus. Unfortunately, there is no way to express this "cloud-top" experience that goes beyond the "mountain-top" experience.

We talked about whether or not God might want to use me to

minister to other cardiac patients, their families and the staff of HVI. Clergy cannot adequately identify with these patients unless they've been there.

Volunteers cannot always represent Jesus in the realm of God's presence and desires for people. Not everyone is equipped to be dispensers of grace and mercy.

Thought questions:

> Could the Father be preparing me for a new direction in life and ministry? Jeff, Randy and I have pondered this question many times.

> Could I be super-imposing my desires upon the Father? Only time will tell.

One of the nurses, Jamie, brought a wind gel sign, "Today is Awesome". She said she wanted to bring cheer into my life today and she did. I felt such a love and appreciation that I hugged her and gave her a kiss on the cheek. The Father is using many avenues to comfort me. I await in wonder at what He's going to do next.

June 11th Today marks seven (7) weeks in ICU. The doctor put in a new swan line yesterday. I was fearful that Dr. L. would have to puncture my neck again, but instead he used the old for the guide to place the line. It didn't hurt much, just the stich to hold the line in place.

Karen spent the day yesterday. She took videos of the procedure. After all of this Karen will become a transplant nurse?

Today's Scripture that I sensed God speaking to me: "I truly believe I will live to see the LORD's goodness. Wait for the LORD's help. Be strong and brave, and wait for the LORD's help."

(Psalm.27:13-14)

"Disobedience is as bad as the sin of sorcery." (1 Samuel 15:23)

"Then all the world will know there is a God in Israel!" (1 Samuel 17:46)

My prayer: Lord the only giant I face is the failing heart. I know if I wait, You will be glorified and I ask You to glory Yourself in the way you chose, but I also ask that the world may know there is one God.

Today two nurses came into my room about beginning a Christian-based support group for patients for prayer and Bible study. They seemed excited about the possibilities.

June 12th Sony (p.m. nurse) came into my room and she was beaming with excitement that I could tell that God is at work in her. She wanted to pursue the conversation we had last night and learn more about how to teach her children about God. She gave the usual, "I'm so busy, work gets in the way & etc." I asked her if she was going to see her life too busy to bring her children up in the Lord and watch their life waste away in unbelief and failure or would she rather give them a boost into eternity.

June 13th Sony came into once again oozing with Godly excitement. She told my morning nurse before leaving that I was the first patient that spoke about God in her career. (Obviously, the morning nurse did not seem receptive or interested.) Sony also told me her husband had lost his job this day. I put my arms around her and prayed for Sony and her family. She gave me her email address, I emailed the chapters to Sony.

June 14th This morning God answered another prayer concerning my blood sugar. Seemingly I have been the one concerned about my blood sugar. Dr. L. and team came in, said something about my nurses' unhappiness about my blood sugar. I told him no more than I am, it's my blood sugar and it's never been this high and I've been trying to talk with someone for seven weeks, but no one seems as concerned as I am. A short time later two Endocrinologist came in. They're putting me back on Invokana – today. They explained there was a tension between cardiology and endocrinology. I mentioned, I had heard that, but this is my body and I'm responsible for it no matter what my cardiologist said.

One of the respiratory techs waited for the doctors to leave. Sonji, the South Korean found out that I'm a Pastor. She became excited.

She explained that she had learned English through the Bible back in S. Korea, but she was a Buddhist. I explained that I am a follower of Jesus and believe in only One True Living God. She told me she was open to hearing more about Jesus, but the people who invited her to church lived one way in church and completely opposite outside of church and she didn't see why she needed to live that way. I told her my story about where would you want a child molester, prison? Where would you want a drunkard? AA or prison. Well the best place for a hypocrite was in church.

I told Sonji that I would be happy to talk further, but I realize she's gotta do her job. I asked her to stop back by and we'd talk further and I would answer any questions. She said she was all alone here in America, her family's all back in Korea. I told her I would be her dad away from home. She was nearly in tears. I put my arm around her & prayed.

Strange, but I sense a deeper hunger and thirst for Christ in the non-Americans (Asians)

Just last night Karen caught me in a funk because of our church's lack of a sense of responsibility for ministry, evangelism and or fellowship. It seems as though four and one-half years had led us to no place different that when we began. It's either can't or won't, attitude. Could the Father be preparing me for after transplant? Could the ministry be to hospital staff?

I truly do not know. I can only ask if this excitement is for here and now or being taken into the future. I have found a true identification with hospital staff. The word "wait" appears again.

June 15th There seems to be a battle of the testosterone's of Endocrinology, Cardiology and Pharmacy. Drs. L. and A. seem to think it is all right to resume Invokana and the Endocrinologist agree. However, Phillip (Pharmacist) came by today with a different story.

Phillip said there's no contraindications of Invokana with the post-surgical drugs, but we will have to wait 'til after surgery to see. So, it seems Pharmacy is just putting me off. The word contraindication means someone cannot take this medicine under some specific condition.

Further development Dr. S (Endocrinologist) said they had it all cleared, go ahead and begin taking it in the a.m.. Dr. N. came in, Leoni told him of the Endocrinologist's and he said, "No." Wait 1-2 months after surgery. They can't seem to agree or make up their minds.

The pacemaker has been showing 99.999% heartbeat stimulation. At 1:50 p.m. the heart begin beating without stimulation 99.999% of the time. What's going on? In the weeks prior, the pacemaker was aiding my heart to beat and its rhythm.

I know that everything is the Lord's battle. In addition to the heart, I've made my request to heal the heart and diabetes. My Scripture reading dealt with Saul's determination to have David killed and how the Lord was with David. The Psalms were about David's prayer of distress and his appeal to the Father for deliverance and healing.

Leoni, a nurse, overheard Dr. A. strongly talking with Dr. N. about the Invokana. She urged him to agree because what has been done had not worked. Leoni' said she overheard A. say she has looked up and there's no problem with this med and what I'm on now. Phillip said there was no contraindication between Invokana and the post-surgical meds. Later in the afternoon, Leoni came in and said we've been given the ok and I need to get my meds from home.

June 16th What might the Lord be doing? The heart strip is still showing almost no pacemaker activity, but a normal sinus rhythm. I continue to ask the Lord to hear me about healing the heart and have added the diabetes, knowing full well He is Lord over all of His creation and He, alone, has the authority to command my body be healed.

I do not take for granted that He will do this. But, like the Psalmist said, "What benefit would a continuation of my situation be to You, O Lord, compared to what benefit I can be to Your name if You chose to heal me?"

> Praise be to You, LORD, for You showed Your wonderful love to me when I was hurting and besieged. In my alarm I said, I am cut off from Your sight!" Yet you heard my cry for mercy when I called to you for help. Love the LORD, all you, His saints! The LORD preserves the faithful, but the proud He pays back in full. Be strong and take heart, all you who hope in the LORD. (BJ's Psalm 31:21-24)

Lyantie called to cause havoc because Tropical Storm Bill is wreaking havoc on the coast. We talked about what I've written above. I mentioned a question I have, that is: "Could God be preparing me and this hospital (employees) for a new ministry?

Lyantie mentioned she was speaking to someone last night about this situation and the lady mentioned the same thing. I am not sure if I am seeking God beginning something new or not. I would cherish the opportunity to teach, preach and disciple those God is calling unto Himself. Lyantie and her friend have coveted to pray along this line.

Again, I now pray, "Father, You be glorified as never before. Lord, Jesus I await You." (Hebrews 9:28)

Activity between Drs. L., A. and the Endocrinologist suggest they believe I would be better served on oral. Invokana rather than injectable insulin. Dr. L. suggested that I might be insulin resistant. I have gotten the go-ahead to bring my own Invokana.

Janice the patient "advocate "came around asking if there were any situations or problems with my care, the room, its environment or nursing care. I expressed to Janice (Aunt Flo as I called her) that I have one huge concern and this is that, as the patient, I'm being talked about by the doctors, but never talked to, consulted or even banter. They make their decisions without ever communicating what they're doing. Janice indicated that she didn't think this was right and they needed to communicate better.

June 17th The drug Invokana, which is for diabetes worked yesterday and seemingly does today. My nurse today, Ivette, is to me an advocate like Leoni. She came and told me Drs. K. and N. were discussing that the nurses weren't being forceful in me taking my medications and they did not like that I had refused the insulin.

Almost simultaneously Dr. B. from Endocrinology, entered as Ivette and I talked. He recognized the schism between cardiology and endocrinology. As we talked, Dr. B. stated he understood and wholeheartedly agreed. He agreed that we've got to give the

Invokana time to begin to work. I showed him my log and he was encouraging, uplifting and affirming. I communicated the fact that my regiment worked until coming into the hospital and I've spend the last seven (7) weeks, six (6) days trying to solicit some change in my diabetic regiment to no avail. The doctors have just kept adding insulin, but the results are – glucose level isn't changing significantly.

Dr. S., an Endocrinologist, came in, sat on the bed and wanted to know how the past 24 hours have been. He looked over the log and said he was impressed and the numbers are responding well. He asked about adding a little insulin (10 units in the morning and 2 units after meals for sugar above 150.) He asked for my input and I told him, he was my Endo physician and I am alright with his decision and feel it is right.

I have to admit I am depressed. I have focused on something wrong and I feel as though I'm about to break. I SIMPLY WANT TO GO HOME.

The nurse Nery came into the room to see what Ivette was concerned about. I told her I was tired of being talked about by the physicians, and would like to be a part of their care routine and included in the discussion, after all – it's my body. I also communicated that I do not want the pharmacist, Phillip back in my room to talk to. (He's condescending and not encouraging.)

June 19th The righteous cry out, and the LORD hears them; He delivers
them from all their troubles. [18] The LORD is close to the brokenhearted and saves those who are crushed in spirit. [19] A righteous man may have many troubles, but the LORD delivers him from them all; [20] he protects all his bones, not one of them will be broken. (Psalm 34:17-20)

Lord, although my body is weak, it was conceived in sin. In sin, my body was given a defective heart, which now Your enemy says, this will prevent you from ministering in Jesus' name. The Psalmist said, "a righteous man may have many troubles, but You, O Lord, deliver him from them all."

I confess I have given up, but never upon You. My hope, my future and my joy rest in   You and You alone.

> "They also opened their mouth wide against me, And said, 'Aha, aha! Our eyes have seen it.' This (You have seen, O LORD; Do not keep silence. O Lord, do not be far from me. 23 Stir up Yourself, and awake to my vindication, To my cause, my God and my Lord. 24 Vindicate me, O LORD my God, according to Your righteousness; And let them not rejoice over me. 25 Let them not say in their hearts, 'Ah, so we would have it!' Let them not say, 'We have swallowed him up.' 26   Let them be ashamed and brought to mutual confusion Who rejoice at my hurt; Let them be clothed with shame and dishonor Who exalt themselves against me. 27 Let them shout for joy and be glad, Who favor my righteous cause; And let them say continually, 'Let the LORD be magnified, Who has pleasure in the prosperity of His servant.' 28 And my tongue shall speak of Your righteousness And of Your praise all the day long.'" (Psalm 35:22-28)

In the depths of my despair and down time, I have been brought to praise of You. I have found a deeper praise of You than ever before. You have allowed me to walk in Your presence and I give glory and thanks to You.

You make life and tribulations a joy to walk through. Your Spirit reminds me of Daniel and his three companions as they were thrown in the furnace, how they danced with joy. Father, You have caused me to focus on the joy You have given me rather than the near imprisonment in ICU. You have place people around me that make me laugh, who care for me as a person, who have stopped by to say hello (Megan and Tyler). You have placed me within a new family, one with a new family with new hearts and those who've ministered to these new hearts.

Despite any separation from friends and family, You have given me a new family. Let all people "shout for joy and be glad, Who favor my righteous cause; And let them say continually, "Let the LORD be magnified, Who has pleasure in the prosperity of His servant. And my tongue shall speak of Your righteousness And of Your praise all the day long." (Psalm 35:27-28)

> Father, I thank you for Dr. B., his faith, his voice and his love and devotion for you. I pray, Father, for Dr. B. understands the Messiah and that he may become complete and help his family and friends realize Your great love for them, through Christ, Jesus, Your Son."

Dr. B. told me this would be his last visit, because next week he has to go to another hospital. I hope You might consider connecting us again?!

June 20th Today was ice cream day. Dr. S. came by said "enjoy it we can make up for it with insulin." Karen was here. A good day

June 28th Today I feel bummed out. I am not precisely sure why. I know the Lord, God Almighty lives within me and has and will provide for me. Maybe I am feeling sorry for myself. Nevertheless King Yeshua is to be praised, adored and worship – for He is my Sovereign and Eternal King without Whom life would have no meaning.

This morning I read Psalms 40-42

"Why are you downcast, O my soul? Why so disturbed within me? Put your hope in God, for I will yet praise him, my Savior and [6] my God. My soul is downcast within me; therefore I will remember you   from the land of the Jordan, the heights of   Hermon—from   Mount Mizar." (Psalm 42:5-6)

Asha, my nurse came in and noticed something different and came over and gave me a hug. She said, "I don't give hugs, but I want to hug you." What a Spirit-driven action!

Spent the morning in meditation, reading of the Scriptures and prayer

Prayed for the surgeons to remain busy transplanting two per day until everyone on the floor has been treated.

I went back through this journal re-reading and straightening up the text. I found some reminders about the walk for the past year, how the Lord has provided.

I have found I have good days and dark ones. When I feel down I spend more time in prayer and the Word. I am especially grateful for the Psalms and the comfort I receive from the Spirit of the Living God from His Word.

June 30th   Today's transplant group meeting was extremely revealing.   The recently transplant recipient and the others were describing their walk in heart failure. Each described events over a short period of time in which they suffered heart failure, came in, diagnosed and treated. Yet, I have been nearly without symptoms, even now. The medicines are creating an environment of "near normal" so my situation is very stable, weight is reducing ever so slightly to 101.kg or 223 today.

My walking partner, Chris suffered a setback last night. He spiked a fever so they pulled his swan line. Chris is depressed. We prayed with Cindy (wife) for Chris.

A swam line is an IV that is inserted into an vein at the base of one's neck. It has several ports where multiple IVs can be ran into the vein. This line goes directly into the heart and delivers a powerful concoction of drugs that keep the patient alive until they are ready for transplant.

I also had this line installed. It was removed at transplant.

July 2nd Today marks my tenth weeks in ICU. While I was walking the nurses were goofing off, laughing and cutting up.

While there they strangely asked how long I'd been here and I told them ten weeks today. Karen came to spend the day and night.

I am sure everyone's thinking this "weekend" could be the time. Everyone knows that July 4th is a big weekend because of all the deaths that occur. I'm trying not to focus on the weekend as an opportunity to get a heart. I know that in the back of my mind, I will think about it, but Karen and I've tried to focus on God's provision and God's timing, not our desires.

July 4th Tonight fireworks will be going off all around the hospital and yet I won't be able to see a single sparkler. Also, today would have been my mother's 90th birthday. As I thought of her, in light of my present situation, I realize she did not have the same opportunity that God's given me.

The holidays are big transplant times because of increased road accidents. A friend asked if I am anxious about the possibility of a transplant this weekend? The thought has crossed my mind, but I can't be overwhelmed with the possibility.

Tonight Karen and I sat in the door of our room. In addition to the Hawaiian shirt, I wore my driving cap and sunglasses and while the 7:00 p.m. shift arrived we clapped and welcomed them to work. Most of the employees were shocked. Some laughed. All were caught off guard.

July 5th "I am distressed for you, my brother Jonathan; You have been very pleasant to me. Your love to me was more wonderful Than the love of women. (2 Samuel 1:26)

There are a few people in my life that I give the Lord thanks for this type of brotherly love. (Mark M., Jeff H., Mark P and Lyantie Gayle. These four have been there time and time again, never wanting, always giving. I AM THANKFUL TO THE LORD FOR THE JONATHAN and DAVID EXAMPLE OF BROTHERLY LOVE.

Today, I long to worship the Lord with tambourines, trumpets, drums and shout unto the to the Lord for His mighty power and His great love for us. What a Warrior He is! I can only celebrate the Lord in my mind and heart because of physical limitations prohibit public worship.

At the same time, I have deep desires within me to help the staff and patients see God Almighty as I have been seeing Him – the Great Creator, the Great Provider, the Great Warrior and my Lord.

I still consider the possibility of beginning a "Healing Fellowship" of hospital personnel, to help them find a real and personal walk with Christ, to deal with the issues of their lives, to give them hope and celebration that they can in turn take back to their patients, who are from all walks of life and nationality. I prayed, "Father give me direction in this. I ask for Your will to be done, in my life, not my will."

4:00 p.m. Dr. A. came in. and told Lauren and I they have an offer of a heart. Later, Sarah, my Transplant Coordinator informed me it was a "high risk" heart, meaning it had a large amount of recent transfusions and or spent some time in jail, but she wasn't in jail now.

July 6th 2 a.m. The nurse came in at with a schedule of 5:30 a.m. for the operating room. The heart hasn't been visualized, yet. We will know shortly about the visualization of the heart. We will have to call everyone.

While this heart may be a good heart, the question of "risk" caused me to prayerfully seek the Father's mind.   We had been praying for a healing, but always in mind He may choose to use transplant. Yesterday I prayed, "Not my will, but Your will". So, we are less than four hours from reporting to surgery.

I recognize the Father still has an opportunity to glorify Himself through healing, but I cannot help but recognize that He has led me to this place and I have chosen to walk across the river at this particular point.

I suppose there is always a small amount of questions, but my mind is settled. I pray for the family of the donor to know Christ and He would give them peace. I pray for my children to fully grasp the relationship with the Father, too.

July 6th 2:oo a.m. The entire family was gathered a second time in my ICU room for the news about the heart and when transplant would occur.   We looked like some type of mountain family camped out in a one-room cabin.   Lauren and Mark trying to get a few Z's on the window couch. Sean slumped in a bedside chair using some electronic device and Karen snuggling with me.

This wasn't our first rodeo. Two previous by-pass surgeries, and numerous trips into the catheterization lab over nearly 28 years was only preparation for this day. Years ago a cardiologist told Karen and I that all the procedures were only stop-gap fixes until one day a permanent solution or transplant would occur.

This thought had been before me for years. Usually the thought was so far back in my mind that I usually did not even think about it. The thought never made me anxious or worried. For some reason the peace of Christ surrounded me.

The prime thought upon my mind and heart was that my life was to glorify my Lord, Jesus with every ounce, every molecule and every organ no matter what anyone else thought or felt. This may seem calloused, but I discovered that spiritual stubbornness was a reality and truth in the life of Jesus, Himself, the Apostle Paul and many others. Paul called it "single-mindedness". Scriptures describe two different views. The first is a person with a double-minded attitude:

> "Consider it all joy, my brethren, when you encounter various trials, knowing that the testing of your faith produces endurance. And let   endurance have its perfect result, so that you may be perfect and complete, lacking in nothing. But if any of you lacks wisdom, let him ask of God, who gives to all generously and without reproach, and it will be given to him. But he must ask in faith without any doubting, for the one who doubts is like the surf of the sea, driven and tossed by the wind. For that man ought not to expect that he will receive anything from the Lord, being a double-minded man, unstable in all his ways." (James 1:2-8)

Paul called a double-minded person unstable in all his ways. Can you imagine being a human rat caught up on a maze? Running and running and never getting anywhere? This person is unable to make a conclusion or make up their mind. These people run from idea to idea, perceived truth to perceived truth, or every promised benefit that can be invented in a television commercial but a single-minded person knows where he or she is going. This person knows what God wants of them. They may not know where their life is going tomorrow, but they know who guides them. This person is determined!

July 6th 6:00 a.m. The transplant unit nurses came into the room and said, "The transplant team is on the way to take you for transplant." Many nurses worked feverishly to prepare me and the IVs for transport to the operating room. There wasn't much personal family time, but my children looked on as if they were saying, "What will happen to him?" Karen leaned over the bed to hug me and kiss me and we both said to each other, "See you on the other side."

We used the term "other side" in two ways. First, the other side of surgery when eyes are open, brain is working again and I can see and hear my family and friends. The second way we used it had an eternal meaning. We all had to face the fact that transplant may not work because of other unforeseen problems or even rejection. The other side for Karen and I meant, "On the other side of Glory in the presence of Almighty God."

As the surgical staff rolled me from the room, down the hall toward the elevators the transplant floor staff gave me a "high five", some wept, some hugged, but every patient becomes family and there's a mixed emotion of sadness and celebration on a unimaginable level.

Return from surgery as told by Karen

Around 11:00 a.m. Karen received a phone call from the nurse with a positive report. The nurse allowed Karen to hear the new heart by telephone. The surgeon gave Karen a video with the heart beating in my chest and when the surgical team returned me to the room, Karen said, "I was covered from the waste to my neck in bandage and tape covering my still unsecured chest incision. My chest incision was not closed for forty-eight hours.

The cardiologists were concerned because the heart monitor kept spiking. They spoke to each other but in front of me. Billy was in an out of his coma but couldn't speak because of the aspirator. He would awaken when doctors came in. Boy, could he recognize the voices of the people who were in taking care of him. He would write messages to me, but couldn't see what he was writing, because of the position of laying down. We tried putting up the alphabet for him to make words, but he got frustrated because it was so slow. I reminded the physicians that he wants to be a part of the process, so they will have to speak as though he were aware completely. They didn't really understand that he was coherent through the induced coma.

That night, about 9:00, they wanted to ablate the heart to stop the spiking. I was surprised because the nurses said they didn't do much after 7:00 p.m., but they must have been somewhat concerned. They came back from the lab and were puzzled because they couldn't create the heart map. They kept reassuring me it was a "good heart" and I believed them the whole time.

God was holding the new heart in his hand, although it was in his chest. Billy told me that afternoon that he wanted me in the room with him and I should check out of the motel. He told Lauren she could leave, since she was 4 months pregnant. He did this by motioning only but I knew what he was saying. As I slept on the couch-bed, I remember being very aware of the nurses giving constant care and walking around the room, but knowing that the room was filled with God's care and His healing hand. It was an unrestful night because of the movement and noise of the machines, but I do know I was calm because God is the Greatest Physician of all.

The next day Billy went through hot flashes. He needed to have ice and cold compresses along with fans constantly. This went on for nearly 3 days. The heart kept spiking, and they kept watching. Later the "cold flashes" could turn to "hot flashes".

A group of medical students from Slovenia were coming in and out of the rooms to observe the physicians. They were very kind and quiet. The physician they were following said suddenly on Saturday, "Wait, I remember I read something about this- thought for a moment and told the nurses to put the bed in a chair position". The nurses did as they were told and almost immediately the heart went into the proper beat. She was so happy she beamed. Billy still had the aspirator, but gave her the "thumbs up" when everyone realized that she solved the mystery of the spiking. The professionalism of the cardiologist team never ceased to astound me. I had so much confidence in them, knowing that it was God who was working through them.

8 LIFE WITH A NEW HEART:
GOD'S BLESSINGS

At this point, the past nearly 36 hours has been the beginning of a new life. My old almost completely dead heart was gone and God had given me a 19 year old heart. Some lifestyle habits would change, some food preparation would change, some places I could no longer go, such as huge gathering where there could be a lot of germs in the air.

There was so much more to change with this gift of new life that God had given me, too much for most people to grasp. But what blessings flowed and have continued to flow.

July 7th 4:14 p.m. by Karen

> The Other Side: Day 2. First, thank you for your prayers. Faith is the victory that overcomes the world! He went back to surgery to close his chest and he has not yet returned from recovery. We are in a hospital so we all know time is relative....sometime today. Although he is on a ventilator, he is on twilight meds and can communicate. Being the teacher, I found a blank sheet of paper and bummed a Sharpie from the nurses and wrote the alphabet on it so he can point to the letters to tell me what he needs. He's being very good and patient with the situation. I am so very proud of him!

July 7th (continued) – 9:48 p.m. by Karen

> "The Other Side: Day 2 - We have been waiting all day for surgery to close his chest. The nurses assured me they do not do surgery after 8 p.m., but they rolled him out about 20 minutes ago. The surgery will take about 2 hours. If you are wondering what to specifically pray about, please ask God to spare Billy from rejection as much as possible

94

and that he will have the motivation to get moving as soon as the doctors give the "OK". Please also pray that the steroids do not make him stressed. They give him so much that it will make him shake like Parkinson's disease for several months and could either make him very depressed or highly agitated. The social workers and nurses staff have warned me for months to be prepared for this and it is up to me to keep him stable and calm. I have been warned to remember the steroids are talking, not him and anything he says that sounds hurtful is not him. I have to be the one to calm him and take it and move on. I know that sounds like a great burden on me, but as the wife, the staff will be counting on me to be the "buffer" and motivator. Please ask God to spare him all this so he can move on."

From Larry (my loving brother) via email:

"This is the day after your surgery. You are still out and the Doctors are waiting to bring you back out of the induced coma. Everyone has been pulling for you. I am so happy that everything went so good :) you have been an inspiration to all of us. You will always be my big brother and hero. I love you... Me :)"

July 8th 12:17 p.m. by Karen

"The Other Side: Day 3. He slept well, but depended some on oxygen, so they are leaving the ventilator for a while longer. The heart is connected to no nerves right now, so as it sends its synapses, there is nothing to receive the message, so it goes into a slight spike in the rhythm at times to figure out what to do. They have him on no heart meds and it is still trying to do it. The doctor looked at me and said, "It's a great heart, very strong willed!" Evidently this happens periodically, so they have to go back into surgery and burn the nerves that are sending the messages. It could take a year for the nerves to completely work for recipients. Until then, he (and all recipients) has no flight or fight reactions. He is still slightly sedated to keep him calm. It's the "honeymoon" period, so the new heart is getting used to its new home. More later as I get info. Still happy, hopeful, and thankful! But very, very, tired. I'll be catching some Z's in a second."

I am adding supplementary information, afterwards, on the nerve issue. When a child is born his or her vital organs are connected to the "central nervous system" by nerves. The brain functions to regulate the heart, lungs and others.

In a transplanted heart all nerve connections to the "central nervous system" are severed. The heart does not beat with any assistance of the nerves. It simply beats independently through chemical reactions.

From Larry:

"Hey bubba.
It's another day and they closed you up last night. By now you may have the ventilator aka.. damn contraption finally removed. I know there is still a long road. However we are past the tall hill and coasting downhill. I know you will be sore. You will start your steroids. However each day should get better.

Email from a fellow seminarian and friend to Larry to pass on to me:

I miss being able to talk with you. So I'm send this email to let you know I'm thinking if you. Your friend Bob sends his best. Love you."

July 10th 9:46 a.m. by Karen

"The Other Side: Day 4 (1 day late). Billy is well. They should extubate (take out the ventilator soon). He was not breathing all the way down into his lungs and they feared it was a collapse or embolism. They took him yesterday to the nuclear lab and did a sonogram, all is well, so they sat him in a chair position in the bed for the day to help him breathe. Slowly, he began doing a better job. The heart is good, they reassure me, but there is a problem and these things happen. In layman's terms (remember, I speak 2nd grade), the new heart keeps spiking beats at about 240 for 10 seconds or so. As of yesterday, it had done this about 10 times. The doctors explained that sometimes 20-30 year olds don't know they have a heart issue, and this was one. They originally scheduled a surgery for Monday to explore the heart, make it mimic the high fluttering and burn the nerve areas that are causing this fluttering. She said after much thought, she rescheduled for today (Friday) because she is concerned there may be an issue this weekend. So, around 2:30 today, please pray for Billy and the doctors. He is still in and out, but alert when he needs to be. He asked (wrote) very good and logical questions to the doctors and expects them to talk to him when they visit and give reports. ME: Yesterday was not so good for me. I suppose I am tired and the adrenaline has worn off. On the way home, I was at an odd, offset intersection and touched the side door of a car. There is more damage to mine than hers, but only a minor scrape to ours. I decided then I need to go to bed. Everyone is okay, I just wounded my pride. I haven't had an accident that was my fault since I was 25. Luckily, she was a nurse at the hospital and was very sweet and kind. And we have the same insurance. Let's hope Liberty Mutual stands up to their commercial promises!

Before you say it, I will be careful and get rest. (but thanks, anyway) Today is a new beginning! Praise God!"

When the doctors began to allow me to come out of the cloud I remember only a small amount of details. However, one detail I remember vividly is the endotracheal tube.

There was this rigid tube going in my mouth and it reached down into my throat. This was the device hooked up to the respirator. The endotracheal tube was extremely uncomfortable. There were times the natural cough reflect would be present and I wanted to cough.

I remembered, even in a half groggy state that same experience after my first by-pass surgery in 1996. While awakening in post-op I began having panic attacks because I could not clear my throat or cough. The nurse came over to the bed and said, "Mr. Jernigan, relax and allow the machine to take care of you. You will have to relax to eliminate the natural cough reflex."

Coming out of the transplant fog, while on the respiratory, I remembered what that post-op nurse told me 19 years before I had to keep reminding myself to relax. Relax! Relax! It worked.

While intubated I obviously could not speak. Karen got me a pad of paper and a pen to write what I was trying to say. Yeah, right! I felt like a five year-old. I couldn't think clearly enough to write or write in a recognizable language. She ended up asking me questions like, "do you want a wet wash cloth?" I would simply nod yes or not. I know we both remember how frustrating, but funny.

July 11th 9:46 a.m. by Karen

"The Other Side: Day 6. What a difference 24 hours make! Early this morning, Billy was set free from the ventilator, 1 chest tube and was put in the recliner chair. He was told to only stay for 2 hours, but he did so well, he stayed for nearly 10 hours! He is on liquid foods, will begin with some solids tomorrow. No shaking from the steroids, no mood swings as warned. His voice is getting stronger by the day and the surgeons and doctors are very pleased with his progress. He spent the day visiting with his brother, Larry and Sister-in law, Lisa and our daughter Lauren. We laughed and goofed around the best we could. Since he has been sitting up in the bed, there have been no spiking of heart rates! He should be up and walking tomorrow. I knew the moment I heard Dr. L.'s sweet voice wake me from a sound sleep this morning in the hospital room and he said, "Extubate him", it would be the start of a great day! Thanks for you praying with me. My God will supply all my needs according to His riches in glory! He gets all the praise and honor!"

July 12th 1:39 p.m. by Karen

"Another morning of excitement. First words heard today again from Dr. L. saying, take out all tubes, send him out to Intermediate Care. We are very pleased! Request: Please pray for Chris, who has been in the same situation, but he's only 42 years old. The family has agreed to ask my prayer family warriors get on their knees for him. He suffered a stroke in the brain early this morning. Fortunately, they were able to extract it early, but he will have to recover. The nurses came to me as soon as I woke up and asked to be with his wife, Jenny. Please pray for God's healing hand and for these two who love Jesus and are learning more about faith in our Jehovah God.

July 13th 5:46 p.m. by Karen

"The Other Side: Day 8, Week 2. STEP DOWN TO INTERMEDIATE CARE!!!!!! Much quieter room and atmosphere. His first heart biopsy came back negative. NO REJECTION!"

July 17th by Karen

"The Other Side: Day 11: Lesson 1: You cannot truly get any sleep in a hospital. Lesson 2: Living out of the trunk of the car for your major things is not fun. Lesson 3: The Memorial Hermann Plaza parking garage can be a fun vacation spot if you get close to the elevators (Never in and out of a hot car, no rain, etc.) Sometimes at night, I sneak out of the room and find a choice parking spot......shhh, don't tell anyone! Lesson 4: My little hand rolling crate is the best thing ever invented (Thanks, David). Lesson 5: There is no lesson 5, I just wanted to keep your attention smile emoticon."

Some of you may have wondered what I mean by "The Other Side". The nurses here use that saying for post-transplant. Words said before surgery as they came into the hallway and waved at him being rolled to surgery was "See ya on the other side, Mr. Jernigan!"

Billy walked around the room by himself today! Getting stronger and stronger!

Thanks for always praying and keeping your interest in my posts. I started this mostly as a journal to myself and an update for others. Your encouragement is overwhelming!"

Email From Geoff, a close friend and a brother in Christ

I found this in Ezekiel, "A new heart also will I give you." I always knew you took God's Word seriously, but you have gone the extra mile. I have never known you to be a person who rejects others, so don't start with your new heart. We are praying for you, Karen and family. It sounds like you have associated yourself with some of the best people on this planet. God bless you my covenant brother. We love you guys and can't wait to see how God uses you in the future.

Email from Tomi, a close friend and a sister in Christ

"Congratulations on the progress. I want to assure you this email is the return to ministry. No waiting for someday! It is here! The ministry that God has given you does not always involve getting out of bed. It may be as simple as communicating with others as your strength returns what God is doing in the midst of all this. HE is your strength and you know that but others need to live vicariously through your words of healing and hope. NEVER underestimate the impact - you will never know this side of heaven.

Prayers for your CONTINUED ministry to be satisfying and as always self-sacrificing as you have proven over and over and over!

Blessings, TL"

Email from Jeff, a close friend and a brother in Christ
"[6] A delegation from the tribe of Judah, led by Caleb son of Jephunneh the Kenizzite, came to Joshua at Gilgal. Caleb said to Joshua, "Remember what the LORD said to Moses, the man of God, about you and me when we were at Kadesh-barnea. [7] I was forty years old when Moses, the servant of the LORD, sent me from Kadesh-barnea to explore the land of Canaan. I returned and gave an honest report, [8] but my brothers who went with me frightened the

people from entering the Promised Land. For my part, I wholeheartedly followed the LORD my God. ⁹ So that day Moses solemnly promised me, 'The land of Canaan on which you were just walking will be your grant of land and that of your descendants forever, because you wholeheartedly followed the LORD my God.'"

¹⁰ "Now, as you can see, the LORD has kept me alive and well as he promised for all these forty-five years since Moses made this promise—even while Israel wandered in the wilderness. Today I am eighty-five years old. ¹¹ I am as strong now as I was when Moses sent me on that journey, and I can still travel and fight as well as I could then. ¹² So give me the hill country that the LORD promised me. You will remember that as scouts we found the descendants of Anak living there in great, walled towns. But if the LORD is with me, I will drive them out of the land, just as the LORD said.

I CHALLENGE YOU MY BROTHER TO TAKE THAT MOUNTAIN! YOUR STRENGTH WILL BE BACK SOON!"

My closest friends, brothers in Christ and fellow ministers sent messages from God's heart. Then, as in today, I read these and weep. The weeping is never from sadness or depression but in awe and thanksgiving.

July 18ᵗʰ by Karen

The Other Side: Day 11. "The doctors are saying there is a strong possibility he may come home late next week.......GULP..........Can't say I'm just not a little bit nervous! Just to name a few frightening realities: Mask wearing, cross contamination safeguards x 1,000, clean surfaces with alcohol spray instead of bleach or chemicals, hand sanitizers at all times and everywhere we go; 15 medications a day at certain times, what he can and cannot eat for the next year and possibly the rest of his life, and that is just to start!

No salad or fruit unless we specifically clean it, no fast food because of possible lack of preparation, no cold cuts unless cooked (which defeats the name: COLD cuts), none of that good moldy cheese like Bleu or Roquefort (we love that), watching meat and any food temperatures like a madman, keep the dogs spotless, no holding the new grandbaby for 1 month after vaccinations, no handshaking, no hugging, no driving, heart biopsies each week for 3 months, then 1 every month for a year, watching for the slightest sign of rejection, sickness, etc. This journey is NOT over. This journey has just BEGUN. I am told it will get better, but this is very intimidating. Look at your average Mexican food dinner: Lettuce, tomato guacamole, salsa, picante......out of the picture unless it is made at home by us only because of Listeria. We were told that food poisoning and Listeria could make us sick, but could kill him. Funny enough, they said he could eat food in a school cafeteria..... hmmmmm......I guess after all the rules, eating out at school could be a consideration..........frown emotion.

Prayer request: There is one chest tube that is still in and must be out before he leaves. Please pray that God heals this pocket of fluid that just won't stop. Thanks!"

July 25th

July 16th was my twelfth week in the hospital. Last weekend the cardiologists were saying they were pleased with my recovery and they are only waiting on the last chest tube to come out. They have x-rayed and examined my chest every day for a week and say, "any day you will go home." Every day comes and goes and it is day by day.

The wait to go home may sound superficial, but after three months, going home is important. This wait is not as crucial as the long wait for the heart, but it is still important.

The last chest tube out. Dr. N.'s visit revealed that after 24 hours post chest tube, pending the outcome of the heart catheterization, I would go home about 6:00 p.m. on the 29th.

Barbi and I had a side bet long before surgery. I bet her a steak dinner I would be going home within ten days of surgery. She said there was no way. It would probably be at least two weeks. She came in just before I went home and said, "We were both wrong!"

July 29th Heart catheterization was a walk in the park. No pain! Heart function up from last week's 5.4 to this week's 6.4. Dr. N. came in about 6:00 p.m. and told me the heart was in rejection. Rejection is either in stage 1, 2, or 3. Mine was a 2. So their plan is to give a huge dose of steroids by IV for the next 3 days and then release me.

August 4th How blessed am I? I received a heart transplant in 74 days. There are several here on the unit that have gone so far downhill that they are having to be put on LVAD. This means if they are to receive a machine implanted in their chest, they will have to be cracked again for heart function. Too, I am thinking that I have not waited all that long, but God gave me mine in time.

While I have been post-operative for 28 days now, I am getting stronger by the day. By the grace of God I am able to walk (with some assistance) and as times goes the discomfort of the chest and shoulders will disappear.

Tomorrow is my fourth post-transplant heart catheterization. I pray that it will have negative results. I'm ready to go home and look forward to returning to church Sunday.

August 5th Heart catheterization resulted in a 1R, not dangerous but needing to be watchful. The nurse came in about 5:30 to prepare us for dismissal. I cried like a baby because God gave me freedom. Francois came in hugged me and prayed for me.

Organ rejection is measured on a scale of 0 – 3. Zero means the patient has no rejection. "1R" is light rejection. "2R" is moderate rejection. "3R" is serious and critical rejection.

Nothing is done medically if a patient is in "1R", but for "2R" the patient begins to receive massive doses of IV Prednisone, which is a powerful steroid. This treatment last for 3 days.

Three days from now is the 27th anniversary of my first heart attack. God has brought us a long way, eight heart attacks, 2 by-pass surgeries and a pacemaker to end up with a relatively short stay for transplant. Nine and ½ weeks from entrance to transplant and four and ½ weeks post-operative.

What a time of God revealing Himself and providing me a picture of Almighty God I probably would not have had. Like Jonah and others, I had to get desperate to see the Almighty.

As the nurse pushed me in a wheelchair and we turned the corner to go toward the bell and out the door to go home I witnessed a plethora of nurses waiting at the end of the hall. Every person who had touched my life, from two shifts, were there to see me off. Have you ever tried to man-up and control your weeping and tears? I couldn't! It was a time of great emotion because I've come to appreciate and love them very much. God had indeed put me in a place for a time I could never have expected.

This crowd was my new brothers and sisters. I was rolled out the door into a new life. They saw me "just as I am" without one stitch, in the suit God gave me at birth. There's nothing more humbling than standing there while a nurse wipes your backside.

When a transplant patient leaves for home the staff do a huge cheerleader send off. While the entire transplant staff experiences disappointments, they also see victories and they celebrate the victories and maintain a great attitude to keep the patients moral high. It takes a special person to work on this floor. Some like it and make it while others don't.

In contrast to my strong desire not to be in the hospital, I now faced leaving the very place where people loved me unconditionally and truly showed care and concern. Now I would have to return to the reality of my life.

Words are not adequate to describe the family connection Karen and I made on the 5th Floor of the Heart Vascular Unit of Memorial Hermann Hospital. We all became family. We loved each other, encouraged each other, prayed with each other and faced each situation together. I will never ever forget the way God connected all of us together.

9 A NEW NORMAL WITH GOD'S GIFT

Normal is a relative concept. What's normal for one person is not normal for everyone. What was my old normal is gone! I have been told I have a new normal, one that I have not yet realized.

We thought of stopping by Dairy Queen! The pharmacist brought in the very large sack of go home meds, it was a shopping bag full. They told me I'd have to eat when I went home, so I asked what. How could I eat with all of my stomach filled with medicines?

It wasn't that bad, just a new routine with all new medicines that had to be taken on a strict schedule to prevent rejection.

In the months leading up to hospitalization, I remembered telling Dr. L. I did not want my address to be 6411 Fannin, which is the Heart Vascular Unit. I also remember thinking this was a serious detour of my life and work. But there has always been something to try to derail, discourage or distract me from that which God called me. Dr. L. is my primary transplant cardiologist and now the only physician that attends me, unless he refers me to another specialist.

When we left the hospital I had to ride like a chauffeured man in the backseat, for chest protection protocol, with my wife in the driver's seat. The drive home seemed different somehow. It had been three and one-half months of viewing the outside world from the inside of a sterile hospital room.

When we arrived home I had an internal moment of private tears and celebration. I was back where I live. As we approached the back door Gizmo and Cooper were ecstatic to see me. Karen and Sean had to subdue Cooper because he is a 65 pound loving and active Brittany Spaniel. Gizmo wanted to lick me to death and smell all the smells. I was worried if they'd remember me? Ha!

August 6th Karen and I went goofing off. We first went and got the truck inspected and then went to the courthouse for registration, then to HEB for groceries. Later in the afternoon we went to Ross to purchase some new kitchen knives. Today was a great day. It was the first time I had been outside in the world in four months. I enjoyed getting out and about for the first time in since April 23rd.

I was thankful for the electric carts at the HEB grocery store. The other stops required the walker the hospital sent home with us. I was worn slap out!

I texted Gary who filled in for me in those four months and asked if he would mind me returning to the pulpit Sunday.

August 24th Next scheduled heart catheterization revealed rejection of 2R. I was told to report to the hospital a.s.a.p. We arrived, got settled in and they started the IV with Solu-Medrol 1 gram. This is a drug that will run three times over the next three days, one each day.

August 27th Should have gone home today. Yesterday was the evening of the third day. NOPE! They were concerned with my complaint of left leg swelling. Dr. L. thought the DVT might have been from the time the vein was removed in 1996 for by-pass. I told him I did not think so because it had only began swelling the week before. They did a doppler and found a deep vein thrombosis (DVT) above the left knee, which would have to be treated. A DVT is an abbreviation for deep vein thrombosis or blood clot.

August 28th Finally got to go home. I thought I could have knocked the door off the hinges. Coming home was a trip! The ride itself, every pot-hole in Houston streets found its way to the suspension of our car. Every bump was like being dropped off the top of a roof in a wheel-barrow. This was a time that I wish I had some of the stuff Cheech and Chong used. Wow, man!

Home, at last! After 74 days of waiting for transplant and 31 days post-operatively waiting for tubes to be removed and being treated for an episode of "2R" rejection –arriving at home was a tremendously emotional moment.

I preached Sunday for the second time. Now, begins the time of daily injections in the abdomen, for insulin and an anti-coagulant, for dissolving the clot.

Excitement after the acquisition of something new is natural. Whether we purchase a new auto, a new home, new furniture excitement seems to follow. It's often not that we got something new, but the excitement that the future will bring gives us a fresh new feeling.

.All transplant heart patients seemingly are excited about the future. They are excited about the possibility of going home. They are excited about the reality the process will be over and they are excited about the possibility of having the Swan-Gann line out of their neck. They are excited about what strength, energy and vitality they will have.

The toughest part is the wait. One waits on a meal from the "Upchuck Wagon" that has no salt, no seasoning and no taste. This was my term for the food hospital patients receive who are on a very strict cardia diet. There's waiting on help to the bathroom or bedpan. Patients have to wait upon the doctors, and news of test results and especially the news that a new heart awaits him or her in the operating room.

The word wait, excitement and strength do not usually go together. The Psalmist wrote:

"Wait for the LORD; Be strong and let your heart take courage; Yes, wait for the LORD." (Psalm 27:14)

"Everything God made is waiting with excitement for God to show His children's glory completely." (Romans 8:9, NCV)

I have found the idea of waiting upon the Lord to truly be strengthening, faith-building, refreshing and it fills a person with the depth of God's love. Think about it, God cares for me and you. The Creator of the universe, the Heavenly Father of Jesus, the One who caused Israel to be led out of Egyptian bondage and the same God who displayed His great power and mercy repeatedly over and over again. Today, God's mercy still rest upon those that love Him.

Many who call themselves apostles and pastors seemingly try to convince their followers to rely upon religious hype rather than the power of faith. Some pastors are like T.V. commercials, promise everything, even beyond what God has promised.

One cannot rely upon anything else than the person of Jesus. One cannot rely upon the hype of unrealized promises. Throughout the years, time and time again I have seen the faithfulness of God fulfilled in my life, so it becomes easier and easier to follow Him. There's only one other truth to consider: God doesn't always work the same way twice. He alone chooses how and when He will work.

Seventy-four days waiting for transplant seemed like a long time. Believe me, it felt as if the transplant event would never happen. After transplant when there were a few complications that delayed our departure for nearly another six weeks, it seemed as if the time for leaving would never come. Day-after-day the sun rose and set. Day-after-day I remained in a hospital bed, but I often forgot, it was an ordeal for Karen, too. She never complained and yet many times she would come to my bedside, hug me and tell me she was proud of me. Why, I do not know.

Coming home is always a dream well anticipated. I heard one of the cardiologists tell this story:

> A man had waited many long months for a transplant. Afterwards the man remained in the hospital for months. Complications are always unanticipated, unexpected, unsettling and tough on everyone. The man went home and within days he contacted the heart center with a report of extremely high blood pressure. You might say, "So?"
> Transplant patients are told to keep extremely accurate records to track their progress and to watch out for rejection. Despite his excellent recovery, he was readmitted.

> After a few short days his health returned to stable and he returned home. Within days he was back, and after three or four days returned home again. After a few events like this, the man realized he had become "institutionalize" (like an inmate) and only felt comfortable and safe in the hospital. In other words returning home was a threat to him and this drove his vital signs up. He was most comfortable in the hospital.

Transplant patients are always extremely vulnerable to infections. One medicine lowers my body's production of white blood cells, which arc the cells that fight infection. If you are familiar with AIDS (acquired immune deficiency syndrome)? People with AIDS immune systems have been compromised by a sexually transmitted disease (STD). My immune system is similar, but it has been purposefully lowered to keep my body producing white blood cells and naturally rejecting the heart. While most people's level is between 20 and 40, mine is lowered to 11. So, it is easy to see why I have to watch being around sick folks and in large crowds. Whatever is in the air from a cough or sneeze, I can catch.

A nurse told me one day, "Remember the Blue Bell scare?" Several months prior to transplant Texas' favorite ice cream, "Blue Bell" had contamination of its plant and produce with Listeria. A nurse warned Karen and I about food contamination that could cause grave illness and possibly long hospitalization. She said, "This would make a healthy person very ill, but would kill you!" I do not live in a bubble, I am very cautious.

I have to be extremely watchful for people near me that are sick. Karen took extreme precautions at school since all the little second grade "elves" carry every known cold and flu. Public sports arenas like football and baseball are off my list of places of visits. I have to watch large crowds. Greeting people at church means no hugs or cheek kisses and hand sterilization after shaking hands. You've heard that most sicknesses come from our hands that have touched something or someone with germs. I now wash my hands, like a surgeon, when I go to a public restroom. I do not use my hands to touch anything.

Delays are often unexpected and disappointing. Through the months of August and September I was in the heart-catheterization lab almost weekly for a heart catheterization biopsy. They would numb a small area and insert a heart catheterization either through my neck or the groin. The cardiologist discovered my neck skin and musculature was tough. I told him that was a necessity as a Pastor – to be thick-skinned for all the people that like to insult or make fun of their Pastor because he makes them feel guilty for their sin.

One might think that by-pass surgery and transplant are a lot alike. They are as similar as getting your nails done and a breast augmentation. The only similarity is they are working on the same muscle and they do have to cut your chest open, but that's where it stops.

Obviously, in transplant, the major difference is they take the old heart completely out of the chest. At the same time they're hooking the ends of the blood vessels up to a heart pump machine and it lives for you. So, for a few minutes you are mechanically kept alive. The transplant heart has been prepared, inserted, hooked up, reanimated and like a new radiator on a car – checked for leaks. Unfortunately, they cannot us "Stop-Leak". If everything is okay. the patient is cleared for closure.

I was told long before surgery that the surgeon would not close my chest for 24 hours. This was because at the time of transplant, it was my third time to have my chest "cracked" and the two previous times would leave a tremendous amount of scar tissue along with a high risk of bleeding.

I can barely remember making my second trip to the operating room. The wonderful IV drugs given in surgery render the patient with an "I don't give a care" attitude. Karen tells me that the love of the nurses for me was immense. Usually there was one nurse, per patient, post-operatively, but apparently I had two plus all the people (nurses and doctors) that God placed in my life in the preceding three months prior to surgery. They all took very good care of me and I have to confess, I think I got spoiled.

Karen and I have been back to the transplant floor several times. Every visit we both receive a long line of hugs and kisses. They came to love us and we them. I can honestly say there have been a lot of people that we have loved and been the beneficiary of their love, but never like this.

Karen told Dr. L., "He (referring to me) has the emotions of a woman. He cries when he sees kitty-cats on television and little kids." He told Karen, "Of course, what do you think. All steroids are made from, feminine hormones."

I unfortunately found out that the steroids had other effects, too. They have made me extremely jumpy. Sudden loud noises make me want to jump out of my skin. My temperament has changed too. We were warned that steroids in the high dosages could make my anger level increase dramatically. They did! Little things became Mt. Everest. Someone not picking up after themselves often left me ready to declare war on Japan or the Soviet Union. My recliner was almost like the war-room during the Cuban missile crises of 1961.

In addition to the emotional issues were the neuro-muscular problems. At this moment, my hands still look like I have symptoms little similar to Parkinson's disease. Typing is difficult, texting is impossible. The earliest attempts at both looked like some Russian secret message. The problem is I couldn't decipher it. So, I had to ask everyone to excuse me, but I could no longer text. However, I'd be glad to talk with them. Unfortunately, both stopped.

Another effect of high-dosage steroids was sleepless nights and leg cramps. As of this moment, after nearly a month on this treatment, I finally slept last night and had only one small incident of a leg cramp. You want to talk about relief? The Rolaids commercial ask how do you spell relief, "R.O.L.A.I.D.S.". My spelling is S.L.E.E.P.!

Through the last month of being home, I have seen a lot of changes. People expect me to look like some zombie, but I don't. After the second day at home, I put the walker in the closet and went to the local shopping center to do some shopping. My temperament went super-sensitive and now is on its way back to normal. My appetite went from never hungry to now I get hungry. Dr. L asked me last week how I feel and I told him, "Bored!" He said, "I pronounce him healthy."

The one most important parts of my life during this whole time has been a difficulty in communicating my understanding about my Heavenly Father. Karen and others have caught tears running down my cheek and asked if everything is all right. It is difficult to share that time after time, tears of joy and worship of God Almighty is the only way to express thanksgiving for His mercy and provision.

I was told by one of my cardiologist that there are one million people in the United States each year that need a heart transplant. Only one thousand per year receive a new heart. That means I am 1 in ten-thousand or 1/10,000. The Father put me on the national transplant list on March 6, 2015 and I received my new heart on July 6, 2015. Standing in awe of Jesus is an understatement. Moses saw the Red Sea opened, Paul and Silas had the jail cell busted open, and I have received a heart from a much younger heart. This fact alone showed me that God was preparing the way a long time ago, for me.

Anyone that wants to tell me God doesn't exist is a fool. (Psalm 14:1) My secret prayer, is that the church I serve and others would be able to experience the supernatural, love and provisions of our Heavenly Father through what I have experienced. I know of only a handful of churches that used this time as a time of seeking the Father's face through prayer. The rest just missed out. In fact, through the entire time, I thought the church I serve would be able to see, hear and experience to some degree that which I experienced, but after returning did not see one ounce of difference.

What I did find was indifference. One man, David, from our church was the only person throughout the time that visited me, called me or texted me. David would even bring me stuff, a

Hawaiian shirt – he knows how I like them, plus other things. David's visit, David's conversation and David's concern for me was not only touching and re-invigorating, but a blessing.

In Matthew's Gospel, Jesus said, "All the nations will be gathered before Him; and He will separate them from one another, as the shepherd separates the sheep from the goats; and He will put the sheep on His right, and the goats on the left. Then the King will say to those on His right, Come, you who are blessed of My Father, inherit the kingdom prepared for you from the foundation of the world. For I was hungry, and you gave Me something to eat; I was thirsty, and you gave Me something to drink; I was a stranger, and you invited Me in; naked, and you clothed Me; I was sick, and you visited Me; I was in prison, and you came to Me. Then the righteous will answer Him, Lord, when did we see You hungry, and feed You, or thirsty, and give You something to drink? And when did we see You a stranger, and invite You in, or naked, and clothe You? When did we see You sick, or in prison, and come to You? The King will answer and say to them, Truly I say to you, to the extent that you did it to one of these brothers of Mine, even the least of them, you did it to Me."(25:31-40)

I do not say any of this from sour grapes, only extreme disappointment in the "church," those who say they are Christians and those whose walk and talk don't quite match up. A New Testament professor I had in seminary once said in his South African accent, "If you walk like a duck and talk like a duck, most probably you are a duck!" I continue to pray that the Lord of the Light will open their eyes to see and their ears to hear.

I have seen God throughout my life working in His mysterious ways. I have heard the voice of God to convict me of sin and guilt. I have heard His voice like that of a dove speaking words of peace into my mind. I have seen some events in my life that cannot be explained by human understanding.

I realize I am a child of the Living God. I have been purchased by the Jesus' shed blood on Calvary's cross. I have been given victory over death by His resurrection of Jesus, His Son. I have been called to walk in the path of Jesus, His Son. It is He that gave me my first new heart – centered on Him, His ways, and His purposes. It is God Almighty that chose to keep me alive from my first new heart through eight heart attacks, two by-pass surgeries and a pacemaker. It is He who caused my primary care physician to find the congestive heart failure when the "cardiologist" I did have didn't seem to care enough to tell me because in his word, "I have bad insurance." I believe with every ounce of energy I possess that it is the Lord God that led me to Dr. L. and the heart team at Memorial Hermann Center for Advanced Heart Failure. I believe it was God's plans to have me in the Houston area. Despite my dislike for Houston, He had me here for this, His plan, to continue His servant's life.

Dec. 9 I asked Dr. L. what the pathology on the old heart was. He said, "It was a huge ball of gelatinous tissue."

Oddly enough, this was the 33rd anniversary of the death of my mother who died from the same heart problem. I often think of the possibilities if medical science could have been there for her.

December 11 What a year 2015 has been? The Heavenly Father gave me a new heart and a new grandchild. Eleanor was born December 11. What an early Christmas gift? One I would have missed if the Father had not given me a new heart.

The name Jean has started as a generational name for women in our family. My mother went by Jean. Karen's mother went by Jean and we gave Lauren the middle name of Jean. Now it's my granddaughter's middle name.

December 25, Karen and I decided to take cookies and homemade pastries to the nurses on the transplant floor. We ran into Dr. K. and visited with him in the hall for a few minutes. He seemed to be so pleased to see us. We hugged and he told us that if I had not received a heart for transplant within a few days, I would have had to have installed a LVAD (a heart pump LVAD means "left ventricular assist device). This a pump with an exterior motor and battery with a tube inserted just under one's ribs and goes into the left side of the heart.

I asked him how was I able to do all that walking on the unit and he responded, "It was your faith in God that kept you going!"

To be clear, he shocked me! Here was a man of science and medicine that was not foreign to the thought of God. Instead of crediting his staff's own abilities, he credited God's. I never knew I was that close to death that I'd have to be put on an artificial heart pump.

10 CELEBRATING THE NEW GIFT
AND MY SECOND BIRTHDAY

<u>2016</u>

July 6th We celebrated the first anniversary of my new heart. Today is my second birthday. The first birthday is November 4, the day my mother birthed me. One year ago today the Heavenly Father gave me my second new heart, a physical heart, when Jesus had rebirthed me and gave me a new spiritual heart – His in 1980.

The first three or four days were a blur. There are only fragments of memories with some standing out more than others.

In the past twelve months there have been high mountain experiences and a few valley ones, too.

The doctors have found two DVTs (deep vein thrombosis or clots). The first was treated at home with self-given injections and anti-clotting medication.

The second DVT was found on June 14, 2016. The radiologist was so concerned, he admitted me to ICU on an IV of Heparin. This clot was huge. It extended from my groin to my ankle. Despite all I have experienced, nothing compares the pain of large DVT except a heart-attack.

The next day the cardiologist sent me home on the oral medication (Eliquis). I call this medicine "Elvis", so now "Elvis is now in the veins."

While God makes gifts to His children, our walk with Him does not exempt us from future trials and tribulations. Yet He, alone, is worthy of our continued praise, our obedience and service.

In the Old Testament book of Job we can see this truth in action.

"There was a man in the country of Uz named Job. He was a man of perfect integrity, who feared God and turned away from evil. 2 He had seven sons and three daughters. 3 His estate included 7,000 sheep, 3,000 camels, 500 yoke of oxen, 500 female donkeys, and a very large number of servants. Job was the greatest man among all the people of the east." (Job 1:1-3, HCSB)

This passage shows what a devoted walk this man had with the Lord, God. It is important to understand that Scripture is inspired by God, Himself. This story of Job is not a made-up story from some human, but given by our Heavenly Father. This in mind, this version indicates Job had "integrity". This description was from God Himself. In other words, Job was a man God considered favored not because of what Job did, but because where Job put God in his life. As a result, God blessed Job with a great life. Look at the blessings bestowed upon him.

- He had seven sons
- and three daughters.
- His estate included 7,000 sheep,
- 3,000 camels,
- 500 yoke of oxen,
- 500 female donkeys,
- and a very large number of servants.

Sometimes we experience the mountaintops of walking with the Lord. We walk in the intimacy of the Lord and find victory after victory. We find that we're walking on a spiritual high. Our prayer life is fantastic. That we know we're traveling the path of forgiveness and obedience. Our faith is high and we praise the Father with a joyful heart.

All of a sudden we find we have rolled down to the bottom of the valley and God has abandoned us.

> "One day the sons of God came to present themselves before the LORD, and Satan also came with them. The LORD asked Satan, Where have you come from? From roaming through the earth, Satan answered Him, and walking around on it.' Then the LORD said to 'Satan, Have you considered My servant Job? No one else on earth is like him, a man of perfect integrity, who fears   God and turns away from evil.' Satan answered the LORD, 'Does Job fear God for nothing? Haven't You placed a hedge around him, his household, and everything he owns? You have blessed the work of his hands, and his possessions are spread out in the land. But stretch out Your hand and strike everything he owns, and he will surely curse You to Your face.' 'Very well,   the LORD told Satan, everything he owns is in your power. However, you must not lay a hand on Job ˻himself. So Satan went out from the LORD'S presence.'" (Job 1:6-12, HCSV)

Let me attempt to summarize these verses. Satan came into the presence of the Lord. God asked, "Where have you come from?" Satan answered, "From roaming the earth."   I discovered something reading between the lines.   Satan wasn't giving information, he was complaining because of God's condemnation. He was in essence, "You know where I've been – that dreaded, awful place where you exiled me to."

Because of Satan's complaining, God asked Satan if he had noticed "My servant Job". God bragged on Job. Satan basically accused God of taking care of His "fair-haired" boy, Job! Then Satan turned the tables and blamed God for Job's perfection by saying, "No wonder why Job is so perfect, You have placed a hedge of protection around him." Satan told God, "Remove Your presence in Job's life and watch him curse you openly."

So, Satan began to test Job to see if he would curse God for the trial and tribulation instead of praising God. In verses 14 -19, Job's nightmare began to occur at the hands of Satan's testing.

"The oxen were plowing and the donkeys feeding beside them, ¹⁵ and the Sabeans attacked and took them. They also slew the servants with the edge of the sword, and I alone have escaped to tell you."(Job 1:14-15)

"While he was still speaking, another also came and said, 'The fire of God fell from heaven and burned up the sheep and the servants and consumed them, and I alone have escaped to tell you. (verse 16) While he was still speaking, another also came and said, "The Chaldeans formed three bands and made a raid on the camels and took them and slew the servants with the edge of the sword, and alone have escaped to tell you." (verse 17)

While he was still speaking, another also came and said, "Your sons and your daughters were eating and drinking wine in their oldest brother's house, and behold, a great wind came from across the wilderness and struck the four corners of the house, and it fell on the young people and they died, and I alone have escaped to tell you." (verses 18-19)

In a short time Satan reduced Job's prosperity to dust. This is the point where many people would become angry with God and ask, "Why God? Why did you do this to me?" It is important to note, God did not do this to Job, Satan did!

Simply put, God allowed Satan to test His faithful servant Job. However, God restricted Satan's power over Job. God told Satan, "everything he owns is in your power. However, you must not lay a hand on Job himself." (12, HCSB).   So Satan took every opportunity, but was restricted.

God's power restricted Satan's power and ability to inflicted trouble upon Job. The next verse (20) reveals two truths:

1. God knows His people intimately. He knows what they will do and what they won't do.

2. God protects His children. This does not mean that troubles won't intersect a person's life. It does mean the Father is there with us and will see us through the tough times.

This happens more often than we notice. Look at your life and see if the following isn't true. As long as things are going fine, we're praising God on High and just as happy as a child standing under a money tree. Let things turn sour and see if we forget to honor God through praise.

God's revelation to Satan revealed a truth we should celebrate in our lives, "Then Job arose and tore his robe and shaved his head, and he fell to the ground and worshiped." The key to this verse is why Job mourned the loss of his children, he worshipped Almighty God. Verse [21] disclosed that Job said, "Naked I came from my mother's womb, and naked I will leave this life. The LORD gives, and the LORD takes away. Praise the name of the LORD. [22] Throughout all this Job did not sin or blame God for anything. (HCSB)

Job realized the material goods of the temporal life on earth were temporary and unimportant. His inner character was revealed when he said, "Naked I came from my mother's womb, and naked I will leave this life. The LORD gives, and the LORD takes away. Praise the name of the Lord. Despite Satan's attempts to derail Job's life, God restore all Satan had taken from Job. You can read the rest of the story in Job.

Please do not think I'm trying to compare my life to Job, but, what a blessing God bestowed upon my life in July 6, 2015. My name was listed on the national transplant list in March 6. Seven weeks later I had to be admitted to ICU. 70 days later the Father gave me a 19-year old heart. I've spent a year in complete awe of God's love and provision. Yet, there have been trials despite the blessings.

In April in a non-related routine check- up with the ear, nose and throat specialist, he found I had the infant issue of oral thrush. This was the start of another adventure, one of experiencing non-cardiac road bumps.

After the thrush was cleared a swelling and redness appeared in my left foot. Diagnosis – gout! The swelling and redness caused a great deal of pain. The treatment was almost as bad. They prescribed a massive dose of Prednisone. It worked, but temporarily it was like trying to cure a headache by being run over by a Mac truck.

In mid-June the transplant team made the diagnosis of a thirty inch blood clot in my left leg. There was almost a constant discomfort of a heart attack. This had a limitation of walking. Going from room to room was a major effort filled with pain. I walked as though I had a broken leg and the short journey was very tiring.

Before the clot was dissolved a rash appeared on my forehead and face. Shingles! I never knew Shingles was a neurological (nerve) disorder. Shingles cause pain and itching. Itching wasn't a problem, but pain radiated from mid-forehead around to mid-back-side of my head.

The external signs of Shingle on my forehead disappeared within a week, but the nerve effects of itching, stinging and pain lasted for 5 months. The Shingles also got into my right eye. Despite a thorough eye exam that found no signs of Shingles in the eye, they appeared in the eye about a month later. After two months of steroid and anti-viral eye drops, I finally began to be able to see out of the right eye.

A note – I never had Chicken pox. Blood test proved it. I did have a Chicken Pox vaccine about 5 years. My question was, "How did I get Shingles?

I am not trying to paint a picture of how I suffered, but offer a parallel to Job. God had given me the gift of life with the new heart. Seven months later, health issues arose that could not be anticipated and were not related to anything. Why?

The "why" was not important. I sensed the Holy Spirit leading my attitude throughout this difficult time. As I met with the Lord in prayer, I felt a great need to praise God in the midst of difficulties and pain. The more trials that beseeched me, the more the Father spoke through His Spirit to calm my spirit, encourage my life and to keep me centered in Him.

There were times I expressed my exhaustion with discomfort. There were times I knew the new direction for my life was on hold and God would not move in my life. Like Job, I would have to wait upon God. Many times God moves before we realize we have a need and other times He allows us focus upon Him and not our situation.

I personally found through the past year what Job said, "Naked I came from my mother's womb, and naked I will leave this life. The LORD gives, and the LORD takes away. Praise the name of the LORD."(21) Whether the Father eliminates my discomfort or not, He is all deserving of my praise, devotion, obedience and love. The Heavenly Father had already blessed me through the years with health and life despite eight heart-attacks and two different by-pass surgeries. I live at His pleasure and for His purpose. Besides, what more love and encouragement for future service to Him than a 19-year-old heart transplanted into my chest?

August 8th   Today was my one-year heart transplant heart catheterization. Up to now all heart-catheterizations were right side for output and biopsy for rejection. Today's catheterization was left side to see if there were any problems in the heart's pumping out into the body or blockages. I've faced this procedure so often, I told Karen this morning, "It's like taking my temperature." The Father has given a peace that all would be favorable.

As I waited in the holding room, I noticed the date, August, 8. I realized that 28 years ago I had my first heart attack. I was 33. Seven more attacks would occur over the next 19 years. In each attack, the Lord allowed me to experience His encouragement and love. The events were almost like God was chiseling away all the unnecessary "stuff" in my life. But I found that while God chisels, God loves. In Hebrews 12:6-11, God's Word tells us,

> 6 "For those whom the Lord loves He disciplines, And He scourges every son whom He receives. 7 It is for discipline that you endure; God deals with you as with sons; for what son is there whom his father does not discipline? 8 But if you are without discipline, of which all have become partakers, then you are illegitimate children and not sons. 9 Furthermore, we had earthly fathers to discipline us, and we respected them; shall we not much rather be subject to the Father of spirits, and live? 10 For they disciplined us for a short time as seemed best to them, but He disciplines us for our good, so that we may share His holiness. 11 All discipline for the moment seems not to be joyful, but sorrowful; yet to those who have been trained by it, afterwards it yields the peaceful fruit of righteousness."

11 WHAT IS YOUR LEGACY?

Legacy is something one leaves behind after death. It could mean material goods, but it usually refers to a quality of one's life, what was important to one. For example, one's legacy could be

- They have a large family consisting of children, grand-children, great-grand-children,
- Their families were successful and may include teachers, doctors, ministers, welders, carpenters or attorneys,
- Their family served as ministers or missionaries,
- They used their life to feed the hungry, house the homeless or give peace to a restless soul,
- They used their life to give everyone they met an introduction to Jesus as their Redeemer.

How would you like to leave a legacy to your children, children's children and so on?

The more important question is this, have you come to know God's redemptive love in a way that is so real, so personal, and so unique to you? Do you know for certain that when you die you will be taken into His presence? More importantly, you can be walking in His presence now? All of this you can know for certain if you realize your life before God:

1st biblical truth
> "For all have sinned and fall short of the glory of God" (Romans 3:23)

2nd biblical truth
> "For the wages of sin is death, but the free gift of God is eternal life in Christ Jesus our Lord." (Romans 6:23)

3rd biblical truth

"But God demonstrates His own love toward us, in that while we were yet sinners, Christ died for us." (Romans 5:8)

4th biblical truth

"If you confess with your mouth Jesus as Lord, and believe in your   heart that God raised Him from the dead, you shall be saved; for   with the heart man believes, resulting in righteousness, and with the   mouth he confesses, resulting in salvation, for whoever will call upon the   name of the Lord will be saved." (Romans 10:9-10,13)

Personally, I have found God's redemption through His Son more gratifying than most people on earth or in His churches will ever experience.

God wants everyone to be His child. His love is for everyone. No one is bad enough they can't receive the redemptive and providing love of Jesus. NO ONE!

One day I was meditating on John 3:16, "For God so loved the world that He gave his one and only Son, that whoever believes in him shall not perish but have eternal life.

Two important truths here:

Truth 1 - God loved the world – including Adolf Hitler, and the most evil people the world has ever known. If God's love was based upon you, it wouldn't be faith, huh?

Truth 2 – The biblical word believe is not a head knowledge. It comes from a Greek word meaning faith – a commitment and faith.

God has provided for everyone the opportunity for redemption under the saving blood of Jesus. Redemption is not automatic –

just because you were born into a religious family or done some religious rite. It is available for all who call upon the Lord.

You may not need the second heart, like me, but every man, woman and child on earth needs the **first new heart** that one can only receive through Jesus Christ.

Would you like to receive that new heart? It is too simple to be believable. Pray through the biblical truths I've listed above. Put it first person; I, or me. (Lord I have sinned... and so on)

Ask God to forgive you all sin and commit to give your entire life to Him through His Son Jesus and live for Him.

I would also strongly urge you to find an evangelical church that believes and practices New Testament redemption. If you know someone in that church, tell them of the decision you've made and ask them to help you make the connection during the very next worship service about your decision.

Prepare to be baptized. Baptism is a tremendous experience and one's first opportunity to be obedient to The Light. Baptism is a greatest first step and then to be disciple by a church.

Plant yourself within that church body and prepare to be loved. Warning: not everyone will be as excited as you are. Don't let that worry you. Like many couples who've been married for two hundred years vs. newlyweds. One couple is excited about their future and the other couple is maintaining status quo.

If you have sensed the Lord calling you to redemption and you respond with a simple faith and give all you are to Him, you will understand my excitement about my first new heart.

My first new heart made my second new heart possible.

Lessons I have learned and revelations the Lord has given:

1. God provides when He wants to and how He wants to and not before.

2. God provides not when or how we want Him to work.

3 The Father puts a few people in our lives to encourage, lift us up, and challenging us.

4. The provisions God has made may have been made long before we were born.

5. The Father speaks, but do we listen?

6. The Father provides, but can we see that it is from Him?

7. When we feel we are alone and there's no one else to care, God is always there!

8. Not all who call themselves brothers and friends truly care.

9. Faith is not developed in the absence of problems but in the fire of trials and troubles. We come to know God as we walk with Him and our trust and dependence upon Him grows and grows. That's faith to me!

10. God's revelation is not for our information. (Many say, that was a good sermon or Bible study). God's revelation is for one's transformation that leads to one's participation and God's glorification.

11. The Heavenly Father intends that every born-again person to be discipled or trained in the Word and deed. This will enable one to discover His fullest will for their

life and to discover the blessings of obedience to Him.

You might refer back to September 13, 2014's entry of what I sensed the Holy Spirit saying to me, "Do not fear! Stand firm and see the salvation of the Lord which He will accomplish through you today!" His message from the Lord proved out to be true. It is a fact that if the Lord speaks to you and gives you a message for your life, it is trustworthy. Watch and see!

Ask the Heavenly Father, "Am I glorifying You? Through my service? By my worship? By my witness?

I challenge and encourage you to fully submit to Him, alone and see if the quality and quantity of your life isn't filled with His everlasting presence and provision.

May the Lord bless you as you live for Him.

ABOUT THE AUTHOR

Bill has served as Pastor for over twenty-five years. During his pastorates his God-given passion has been to witness people's spiritual life being revived and filled with the excitement and security of knowing they are a child of The Living God redeemed by His Son, Jesus and given victory over the trials of this life.

He has worked in inner-city missions, international church strengthening and growth, and a volunteer on the heart transplant unit.

He takes seriously Jesus' commandment in Matthew 28:18-20 about going into the world and proclaiming Jesus as the only Savior and making disciples of those who embrace Jesus as Lord and Savior. He has used a long-range disciple making plan for years with a great deal of success and he would be happy to share it with you.

Bill can be reached by email through the ministry website: www.billjerniganministries.org

Visit our website to see the available Bible studies and articles

www.ingramcontent.com/pod-product-compliance
Lightning Source LLC
LaVergne TN
LVHW021345080426
835508LV00020B/2113